FEWER.

BETTER.

AND OTHER BUSINESS LIFE LESSONS

ISBN 978-1-7378542-0-3

Fewer.
Better.

And other business life lessons

Howard Mann

Author of *Your Business Brickyard*

Joe Heller

True story, Word of Honor:
Joseph Heller, an important and funny writer
now dead, and I were at a party given by a billionaire
on Shelter Island.

I said, "Joe, how does it make you feel
to know that our host only yesterday
may have made more money
than your novel 'Catch-22'
has earned in its entire history?"
And Joe said, "I've got something he can never have."
And I said, "What on earth could that be, Joe?"
And Joe said, "The knowledge that I've got enough."

Not bad! Rest in peace!

- KURT VONNEGUT
(First published in The New Yorker, May 2005)

Contents

SECTION FOUR: SALES & MARKETING

SECTION FIVE: RISK AND RESILIENCE

> **"**
>
> IF YOU WANT TO
> STOP CHASING
> "MORE," THEN
> THESE STORIES
> ARE FOR YOU.

Introduction

"To be candid with you, your business has a value right now of nearly zero."

I remember their faces. That stunned and sunken look when someone says something you know deep down but dare not say out loud.

The couple sat across from me in the kitchen of the home they had lived in for over 40 years. They were finally at retirement age, but their retirement savings had disappeared. The couple had spent their careers in the building materials business, always planning to sell their business for a hefty sum so they could then enjoy their retirement.

Their industry had other plans.

The Home Depots of the world had made the couple's business a relic. When I met them, their business had no value. They called me for help on salvaging what they could but I was only able to help them find a modest way forward. I couldn't turn the clock back.

This is how work and business ownership has panned out for far too many. The couple worked so hard their entire careers so that someday they could retire and enjoy it all. This sweet couple had planned for a someday that was never going to be.

My first book, *Your Business Brickyard,* had the subtitle, "Getting back to the basics to make your business more fun to run." I believe in this simple statement more than ever. Owning a business needs to be fulfilling to your life today, not just someday. Deciding work is about hustle, grind and suffering does not allow you to be your best outside of work. When work is set up to be a slog for some later return, everyone in your world loses. You most of all.

The common thread to all of the short business stories in this book is this: **Business needs to be fun (and fulfilling) so your life can be the same.** It needs to be this way today, tomorrow and when you get to whatever payday/windfall/retirement event you hope to have.

Imagine if that amazing couple had not banked it all on their someday. When they started out, imagine if someone had helped them see the reality of this antiquated and broken model of "suffering now to enjoy your someday." I cannot go back and tell them how wrong this approach was and is, but I can tell you and then you can do something about it. To find your enough. Now.

To me, THIS is the true purpose of a business. To provide your level of enough -- financially, intellectually and emotionally -- at every stage of your business's growth and evolution.

Why a Book of Short *Business* Stories?

It has been 12 years since I wrote my first book. When friends asked if I would write another, I would just answer that I did not have something new that I felt would warrant a book. The truth is I did not want to write a traditional 300 page business book. You know the ones, they make their point in the first 50 to 70 pages and then spend the rest repeating it in different ways. The thought of doing that just does not sit right with what I think business owners need.

We all have less time. We all are seeking faster answers.

Most of us do not have time to read 300 pages to see if there is any learning for us. I know I usually don't.

All of this had me thinking about the great writers who create incredible collections of short stories. Bite-sized nuggets of wisdom and thoughts that can be read in 10 to 15 minutes. Some stories may not move you, but a few hit squarely in your head and/or your heart. One or two might actually change the way you think or the way you see your world.

So why not a book of short business stories?

That is what you are holding in your hand. These stories are connected, but each stands alone. They are a collection of the lessons I have learned, often the hard way, about business, strategy and life.

My thinking about business has evolved from the pursuit of growth and wealth to strategies that help your business create a life that is <u>enough</u> for you and those you care about most.

What is enough should be personal to you. I have found that most people have no idea what *their* enough is. The byproduct of this is a relentless chasing for "more" that comes at the expense of your business being truly great at one thing. Never feeling you are enjoying the journey has a serious trickle-down effect on your life.

If you want to stop chasing "more," then these stories are for you.

No More "More"

Let me start by saying something I already know about you: You sometimes feel like a failure.

I know this because I know that there are people in your industry that are doing 10 (or 20) times better than you are. They make a ton more money than you do. They have a bigger home. They drive a nicer car. They already have the life you imagine in your dreams. Based on the ways all the people you want to impress measure success, some of your competitors are more successful than you are.

You also feel this failure in your gut because you cannot help but consume business news and the nonstop drumbeat about entrepreneurs who have created billion-dollar companies, while yours just grows a little each year. Or some years, maybe not at all.

And this feeling that you are not measuring up to this ideal drives you to work even harder. To do more even if it is only that... more.

Somewhere deep in your mind there is this story, stuck on repeat, that you NEED to do more to HAVE more. Your business needs to offer more so you can earn more. Your family and friends need to understand this because this is simply the right of passage for an entrepreneur. This is just what it means to own a company.

More, you think, is what is required to build a business that will finally match that vision of what you think success is supposed to look like... someday.

I know this because I am a failure as well. I joined a CEO peer group 27 years ago when I was running a 150 million dollar business. I walked into that first meeting in my sharp designer suit and tie feeling like a successful entrepreneur who was making a nice and comfortable living. But after listening to my colleagues' stories about their massive business acquisitions, their multiple houses, boats and private planes, I drove home in agony and anger, fuming at myself that I need to be doing so much more.

Those meetings triggered emotions that I would dare not say out loud, and triggered them every single time.

Why can't I have what they have? I must not be doing enough! They seemed to have so much more and I REALLY wanted more.

I never stopped to ask WHY I wanted more but, mannnnnn, did I want it!

Forget that I already was spending less and less time with my friends and family. That this feeling of not measuring up was causing me to be awake half the night.

I spent nearly a decade of my life feeling this way. Until it almost cost me my business and DID cost me my smile. My quest for "more" overextended my business and it overextended my life. In fact, the only way I was able to get off this relentless quest for more was to sell my business.

Not for a big windfall of cash, but just enough to get my life back.

It was only after the sale that I could create the necessary space to see what it had all done to me. What it had cost me. I will forever wish I had stopped drinking the "more" Kool-aid and scaled the business back to what it needed to be so it was enough just for ME.

But this struggle is not confined to just our business lives. In fact, this song of "more" has been stuck in our minds since we were kids.

Remember how your friends always had the toys you wanted? Maybe a bigger house. Maybe they had more friends or the friends that you wanted to be yours. Maybe they simply appeared to have a happier life than yours.

Everywhere we look, it seems, is evidence of someone who has what you wish you had.

If only I could get X or if I could only earn Y... THEN I would be content.

This warped mantra of "I will be happy when... " compels us to keep pushing for more and more.

This has been the embedded brain song of the entrepreneur for so long that we do not have any sense that there is another way.

We do more because we believe more gives us the chance to be more successful and then THAT will FINALLY make us happy.

Because "more" will help us create a life that matches the external picture we see of those that we think are successful and happy.

Along the way, we get enough to buy a home and have a mortgage and all the related life expenses that force us to work even harder, even if we hate what we do each day to pay for the more we have created.

You know as well as I do that once all of those life commitments and related expenses reach a certain level, there is no getting off the ride.

Our entire day becomes filled with a lack of fulfillment and then we come home and expect those few hours to somehow make it all worth it?

It is stressful for me to even say all of that. I know how stressful it is to live it. I am hoping it is now forcing you to feel it more deeply than before.

I am walking, living, breathing and smiling proof that 99% of what you think is the entrepreneur's journey is broken, a bit psychotic and robbing you of the life you could (and should) have NOW instead of that mythical someday.

As I dug myself out of feeling like a failure years ago, I stumbled across a simple two-word formula that helped me never feel this way again. In the next chapter I will share that lesson, and those two words, with you.

"The hardest financial skill is getting the goalpost to stop moving. But it's one of the most important. If expectations rise with results there is no logic in striving for more because you'll feel the same after putting in extra effort. It gets dangerous when the taste of having more—more money, more power, more prestige—**increases ambition faster than satisfaction.**"

- Morgan Housel, *The Psychology of Money*

66

GROWTH HAS TO
HAVE MEANING
AND PURPOSE
TO YOU.

Fewer. Better.

Like someone near the edge of a waterfall waving frantically at oncoming rafts, I have spent the last 21 years teaching a contrarian approach to business strategy so that as many business owners that are willing to listen reverse their course.

As German economist E.F. Schumacher put it, "Any intelligent fool can make things bigger, more complex, and more violent. It takes a touch of genius – and a lot of courage – to move in the opposite direction."

Today, I am here to propose a different way and plead with you to try it. A different tune, if you will, for you to start to sing.

It is a song I have used to transform countless businesses. More importantly, it is a tune that has allowed me to transform the LIVES of entrepreneurs for over two decades.

And the new song has only two words. And those two words are: "fewer" and "better".

Say it to yourself a few times because it needs to become your new mantra.

Fewer. Better.
Fewer. Better.
FEWER. BETTER.

Absorb these words because there is no part of your life that will not improve when you start to do fewer things, better.

Now, I realize that I have just shattered every book about 10X growth you have ever read. I'm ruining your long range plans for world domination and one hundred million in revenue (or some other goal that exists only to feed your ego). But, as famed entrepreneur Ricardo Semler so delicately put it, "Only two things grow for the sake of growth: businesses and tumors."

Growth MUST have meaning and purpose. More importantly, growth has to have meaning and purpose to YOU.

And it HAS to have meaning to the LIFE you want.

When you decide that you are ready to have your someday today, then you need to figure out what is enough for YOU today. Not what is enough for your peer group, or what the last business book you read said you should want, or what the motivational speaker you saw at your last business conference had to say about success.

You need to step off the entrepreneurial pride ride long enough to finally figure out what is enough for YOU.

What is enough for you to be happy today? To feel content, today? To FEEL successful TODAY?

What do you actually need for that mythical someday (instead of the silly 50 million or 100 million targets you picked because it just sounded like an impressive and big number)? A more realistic someday number that will allow you to enjoy the journey TO that someday?

In the mostly forgettable movie *The Gambler,* there is one unforgettable scene. A loan shark, played by John Goodman, gives a compulsive gambler, played by Mark Wahlberg, a lesson about how you create true power and comfort in your life. Wahlberg's character has just lost another 2.5 million dollars after his latest attempt to try to hit it big from a bet.

Here is that lesson:

> Gambler: *"I've been up two-and-a-half million dollars."*
> Loan Shark: *"What do you got on you?"*
> Gambler: *"Nothing."*
> Loan Shark: *"What did you put away?"*
> Gambler: *"Nothing."*
> Loan Shark: *"You get up two-and-half million dollars, any asshole in the world knows what to do. You get a house with a 25-year roof, an indestructible economy shitbox car, and you put the rest into the system at three to five percent and you pay your taxes. That's your base. Get me? That's your fortress of fucking solitude. That puts you, for the rest of your life, at a level of 'Fuck You.'"*

> *"Someone wants you to do something? Fuck You. Boss pisses you off? Fuck You. Own your house. Have a couple of bucks in the bank. Don't drink. That's all I have to say to anybody."*

> *Loan Shark: "Did your grandfather take risks?"*
> *Gambler: "Yes."*
> *Loan Shark: "I guarantee he did it from a position of*
> *Fuck You."*
> *Loan Shark: "A wise man's life is based around Fuck You.*
> *The United States of America is based upon Fuck You.*
> *You're a king? You have an army? You have the greatest*
> *Navy in the history of the world? Fuck You."*

In order to know what YOUR level and position of Fuck You is, you will need to understand what you want out of your business so it is fulfilling for the LIFE you want.

No more. No less.

How much would you like to have in the bank so you are at peace when your head hits the pillow each night? How much will you need to earn each year to create your position of Fuck You?

Not knowing what you want from your business today leaves you left to copy or keep up with someone else's version of success. Or worse, to flounder around unfulfilled for your entire career.

I am willing to bet that the number that creates your position of Fuck You is a lot less than the wild targets and goals you have set in the past. Your number may have fewer zeros in it but it will be far better because: A) It is attainable in the near term instead of someday; and B) It's YOUR number.

Your **Fewer Better** number.

From this Fewer Better number will come more ways to create a life that has fewer, better of everything.

Here are some fewer and better places where you can begin:

1 Focus on fewer, better things each day. Throw out your long to-do lists. Working through a long to-do list every day for years on end is a productivity treadmill. Lots of energy with very little forward movement. Spend more time on what you love to do, where you create the most value and the activities that make you enjoy today.

2 Offer fewer, better products and services. Your business probably offers more products and/or services just to match your competition and not what your ideal clients actually want and value. Reduce your offerings to the few things that you do better than everyone else and watch what happens to your business and its profitability.

3 Employ fewer, better people in your business. The number of people you employ is not an indicator of a successful business. Fewer, better people working with fewer and more valuable clients is the path to meaningful profit leaps so you can create your someday income today. Hiring just to fill seats will water down your offerings while increasing your expenses.

4 Fewer, better "friends." All those social media follower counts and loose connections on Facebook with people you know from elementary school rob you of fewer and better meaningful friendships, deeper relationships with your kids and more time with your family. Why not do a little inventory on all of those connections and figure out the 10, 20 or 30 that matter to you the most? Then, for each one, think about what you will do in the next few weeks to strengthen and appreciate that relationship. Maybe it is as simple as a text, or a handwrit-

ten letter. Or maybe you will jump on a plane to spend some meaningful time together. Do this exercise every month and watch what happens.

5 Fewer, better possessions. What if you could live a more edited life where you had the very best of the things you need, love and will use? Refocus the energy you currently spend acquiring lots of things without much thought and channel that energy into researching the very best of each item that you will use the most. The possessions that light you up, make life easier or are just matter to you the most.

Now it's your turn. As you think about your new Fewer Better world, what comes up for you?

How is the chase for more driving you to a destination you can never reach?

Where in your life could you be doing fewer things better? Journal about it. Talk about it (without pride - see the next chapter!) with the people you trust and care about the most. Create and carry a short list of five areas in your business and life where you could be doing fewer things better. Look at it every morning or right before you go to sleep.

Write "Fewer. Better." on your mirror or on a sticky note on your computer monitor.

Do whatever it takes to get your mind to start thinking about doing fewer things better, and stop that awful feeling of always wanting and needing more.

When you no longer measure your success based on outside stories and what you think everyone else thinks, not only will this feeling of failure disappear but the success that has actually always been hiding in plain sight will be yours.

Fewer. Better.

PRIDE IS AS
MUCH A BUSINESS
PERSON'S ENEMY
AS FEAR. OR
MAYBE MORE SO.

Fuck Your Pride

*"The walls of pride are high and wide.
Can't see over to the other side."*

— BOB DYLAN

In the middle of 1996, I sat down in "the big chair" after being pro-moted to president of a middle size freight and logistics company. More than 140 in staff, six offices and $150 million in revenue flowing in and out of the organization. While that may sound exciting, the real picture was not a rosy one. We were losing money. Clients had gone bankrupt on us (as they fought through a recession), leaving us holding the bag. As an industry flailing in response to the same recession, we were giving away services for less than half of our normal fees. Clients demanded we match competitive quotes. The bank was breathing down my back.

I remember it so vividly. Looking out across my desk was like looking at a landscape littered with business wreckage. So many things urgently needed my attention that it was hard to know where to begin. But more than anything, I felt alone in the battle. Like any competitive industry, if the staff thinks the ship may be sinking they look to jump to another ship. My core team was more than loyal, but human nature is what it is and they had families to feed. So it was up to me to deliver on the challenge, alone.

My friends, old and new, looked to me as a young but smart business person. "I am sure you will figure it out," they said. So how could I tell them about my deep fear and worry? What would they think of me if they knew the truth?

So many things needed to get done. So many things…

I picked up the phone and called a business owner I respected and asked for a referral to someone who could provide candid coaching, support and counsel. Specifically, I said, "I do not want a management consultant that will tell me to buy low and sell high or write some giant report. I want someone who will tell it to me straight and call me out when I am bullshitting myself."

My first call with his recommendation lasted well over an hour. When we were done I asked the two questions that were left to ask: "Can I afford you?" and, "Can I afford not to afford you?"

I made one of the hardest and smartest business decisions in my professional life and spent the money we didn't really have, because getting the company back into the black would be worth 100 times what I would pay the coach. My business, and those that depended on it, were worth that risk.

He supported me as advertised. I now had someone who had been through deep business struggles many times before. I could tell him the naked truth and he wasn't going anywhere. He called me out on my bullshit with candor, empathy and integrity.

Within six months we were back on track. We adjusted our focus and made some smart moves into higher-margin businesses. We executed a plan that had a manageable number of objectives. Within 12 months we were back to profitability.

But here is what is more important: I should have called him two years earlier.

Why didn't I?

I knew the business was stumbling and tried everything I could think of to fix it. But I never asked for help. Sure, looking for some "secret sauce," I talked to marketing, design, PR and communication agencies and paid handsomely for them to build up the facade of a business that deep down I knew was cracking at the foundation.

What I could not see was what so many others also never see until it is too late: It was the business end of the business that needed attention. And very few like to get involved on that side. It's not sexy. The underlying issues are not clear and the outcome is far from certain. There is no "magic bullet" other than grinding work, tough choices and demons to face. But if you are left alone in this battle, you will continue to feel alone. The story ends badly. And it will end.

More than 24 years have passed since I picked up the phone and asked for help. Since the business turned around, we were able to sell it in early 2000. A few years later I hung out my own shingle to help business owners never have to go through what I went through. To help those that are brave enough to ask for help before it is too late. To realize what I have after all of these years -- that most businesses need not fail. I wrote a book and I give keynotes around the world to teach others about what I learned from those tough times.

Having now helped hundreds of business owners, entrepreneurs and CEOs through their own dark times, I have come to recognize one common threat they need to defeat before I could help them. It is the same demon that caused me to lose two years, and my smile, before asking for help. That threat, that demon, is pride.

"Pride makes us artificial and humility makes us real."

— THOMAS MERTON

Please tell me a single thing that your pride will fix or make better. Just ONE. Tell me how pride will help you when there are a dozen critical decisions that need attention and you are only one person trying to figure it all out. Tell me how pride does anything but become what will torment you for many more years after the business is gone (and, I speak from experience here, it will). Pride is as much a business person's enemy as fear. Or maybe more so.

Somewhere pride has become an important piece of armor in business. It does not work. My clients, the ones that asked for help, are some of the smartest and bravest business people I have ever met. They replaced the false shield of pride with one of courage. They dropped their armor. Their businesses are all thriving because they chose their business over their pride.

Don't confuse pride with integrity. I don't care who you call as long as you call someone and tell them the raw truth and, yes, talk about your pride.

In the toughest of times, my pride betrayed me by masking my real fears and kept me alone with my pain and stress.

Well, fuck my pride.

Fuck yours too.

"

"If it's flipping hamburgers
at McDonald's, be the best
hamburger flipper in the world.
Whatever it is you do, you have
to master your craft."

- SNOOP DOGG

BUSINESS IS A CRAFT

IF YOU CARE ENOUGH
TO DEDICATE YOUR TIME
AND SHARE IT WITH
THE WORLD, THERE IS
ARTISTRY AND CRAFT IN
EVERY BUSINESS.

What's Your Craft?

Have you ever learned about a knife maker who lovingly creates every blade by hand? Have you ever watched a video about someone who painstakingly builds custom bikes that may take months to complete? Perhaps you have watched the great Netflix series, *Chef's Table,* and marveled at the creativity and success of the world's great chefs and their lifetime devotion to their craft.

I envy them. Maybe you do as well.

It has made me wonder why we do not think about our non-creative businesses as craft and us business operators as creators of art. We think the goal is to create scale through efficiency and automate everything we can. For a regular business, the skills we talk about are hustle, grind and crushing the competition. That, I am sorry to tell you, is not craft.

Malcolm Gladwell famously talks about needing to spend 10,000 hours on our work to attain mastery. We all romanticize the idea while we spend 20,000 hours just keeping the wheels on our businesses. Then we feel the effect of time but not the satisfaction of mastery.

We could achieve the same -- if not vastly superior -- results, enjoy our days more and create better experiences for our customers if we thought about our businesses and everything we do within them as our craft.

What is your craft?

What activities allow you to put your craft to use?

What things could you do to increase your mastery of your craft?

What would this shift in thinking do to the care and attention you put into every detail of your product or service?

I have the ability to write and communicate, especially if I really take my time to craft my thoughts and ideas. Why would I not want to take as much extra time as needed to craft a proposal that the reader enjoyed as much as a great business book? That's a high bar for a business coaching proposal, but it would turn the grind of writing a proposal into an opportunity to practice my craft. I would deliver a proposal to my potential client that they have never experienced before.

While this is easy for me to say, it is not something I regularly practice. I have the ability to do it and yet I look for a template to copy or I talk about how it is not a valuable use of my time. I am not sure I can believe my own bullshit anymore. It's not helping me or my business.

If you think mastering your craft would impede your ability to scale then you are thinking about this in the wrong way. If you ever watched the movie *The Founder,* about the origin of the McDonald's empire, then you saw this in action and how it led to one of the largest businesses in the world. In a quest to create a hamburger drive-in experience where people would not have to wait in endless lines, the McDonald brothers painstakingly map out the perfect kitchen layout.

Within this optimal kitchen, they choreograph the movements of every employee until it is a symphony of efficiency. For the McDonald brothers, creating this was their joy. It was a full expression of their gifts. It was their craft. They called it their "Speedee Service System." While everyone else was OK running a status quo burger stand, they were obsessed with the craft of refining every element of it. Yes, Ray Kroc used real estate and franchising to go global. But it would never have worked without the McDonald brothers solving a puzzle that their competitors had deemed not worth their time.

So, I ask again, what is the craft of your business? What expertise could you focus on that all your competition only tries to be as good at as everyone else?

How do you express your passion or your expertise? How do you get to turn your business into a craftsmen shop instead of an office?

I do not care if you are an accountant or a lawyer or if you own a trucking company. **If you care enough to dedicate your time and share it with the world, there is artistry and craft in EVERY business.**

Consider Zingermann's

Consider Zingermann's, the famed sandwich shop in Ann Arbor, Michigan. They are world-renowned for their approach to customer service. Lines to buy their food stretch around the block. They could have easily franchised and opened up more locations all over the world. Instead, they have their one location and have grown by creating a business school right next door that teaches other business owners about their approach to business and service. Having one super successful store and a way to share their success with others is enough for them.

Gag Me with Your BHAG

Business is supposed to be fun to run. This core truth has been the through-line for most of my work and career. Through the ups and downs of businesses I have run and for the many clients I have worked with, "fun-to-run" has been the guiding principle.

Just like in a marriage that has lost its fire, not feeling the love for your business anymore impacts your life, leads to flailing strategic decisions and stifling resignation.

So HOW can you make business more fun and fulfilling, so it gives you joy? It is not enough to just want it or lament not having fun. What can you actually do?

The typical prescription is to focus on growing revenue and, more importantly, profit. In many cases, it is the best way to stop a business from losing money, but it stops the bleeding without curing the patient.

I am sorry to tell you that the solution also will not be found in your mission statement, your purpose, your why or your Big Hairy Audacious Goal, or "BHAG," as coined in the book *Good to Great* by Jim Collins.

You probably have done your BHAG exercise. You may have your three-year strategic plan and do your quarterly rocks every month.

Bringing you any joy? Fulfillment? Fun? Yeah, I didn't think so. Never did for me either.

Here is another good one: Figuring out how you can only work ON your business instead of IN it?

This is the ultimate "if only" refrain from so many business owners I meet and the aimless quest of entrepreneurs around the globe. "If only I could make my business a self-running" business." Ooooooooh! "I want to spend all my time working on my business and none working in it." Business nirvana!

I am calling bullshit on all of it.

If your joy is derived from not being involved in the day-to-day, then why are you in that business? I want to propose that what is really at play here is that you are no longer practicing your craft. Unless your craft is creating self-running businesses, or you are unclear about what your craft even is.

How much time do you spend practicing your craft?

When work is no longer fun it is because we are just involved in activities and not practicing our craft. Everything has become busywork. Fulfilling work should not simply feel like being busy.

What is your craft? What, if you could spend all day doing it, would make you smile? What would leave you driving home at the end of the day with real satisfaction about all you did that day?

You have a craft. Even if you just manage people all day, you have a craft that is worthy of perfecting.

To borrow from every infomercial... But wait, there's more! Changing your work into your craft does not mean you drop everything you currently have to do. Any task can be drudgery - or an opportunity to express your craft. Let me give you a recent example.

I was walking with a client back into his office building after a meeting. An office building he had completely renovated and rebuilt. You see, he is a super creative entrepreneur who builds truly remarkable buildings. You might think he is in the real estate business, but that is not his craft.

Electricians were out in front of the building trying to decide where to install power outlets that would charge the two electric cars my client had purchased. They were about to bolt the outlets randomly on the side of the building. My client jumped in and sketched out a creative solution that showed the electricians a better way to practice their craft.

We then walked into the building and one of the younger members of my client's team came running at him with a crisis and papers she claimed had to be signed in the next two minutes. My client stopped and taught her how these deadlines really work and a different way to handle it.

Sounds like a typical day at the office? Not how my client saw it.

He turned to me and said, "You see the stuff I have to get involved with? This is why it is impossible for me to work ON my business."

Nope! What I saw was someone practicing their craft. In five minutes he had taught the electricians a more elegant way to install a power outlet and taught a key member of his team a few important lessons. He was a teacher and coach to each of them in the process.

If he could change how he looked at these interactions, he would see he was practicing his craft. When I pointed this out to him, he smiled (always a good indicator) and said he actually loves doing that type of stuff. Somewhere along the way, he had decided that **doing what he loved was not the role of a business owner/entrepreneur.**

Amidst all the marketing noise and mountains of business books, we have lost the plot about how we spend the bulk of our waking hours.

Was he working in his business and not on it? Perhaps. More importantly, SO WHAT? He was practicing his craft and doing so brought him joy. Many little things about his company were improving as a result. If only he could stop hearing the entrepreneurial echo chamber about needing to create a self-running business with a world-dominating BHAG. Gag me with you freaking BHAG. Please.

What is their craft?

Now take this concept to your entire organization. What is the craft of every single person working for you? Do they know what their craft is and are you encouraging them to perfect it? Do you honor their craft? When someone from your accounting department brings you a spreadsheet that took them hours to create, do you acknowledge the skills it took to create it? When your head of HR/people deals with a tough personnel problem, do you tell them how you admire how they handled it?

When they fail to do their very best, and not treat their job as their craft, do you tell them they could do better and challenge/ teach them? Or do you say nothing or just tell them the work is no good?

Imagine your business filled with people that are continually attempting to do their job (their craft) with perfection. Do you think that the company could fail? Do you think that the company would develop a reputation for being consistently excellent? Do you think revenue and profits would grow?

How do you think it would feel to work in that kind of business, filled with craftspeople? How would it feel to run it? Consider all of the things it would become known for. Consider how it would translate to sales and marketing. The stories you could tell the market. Think about all the ways you would become memorable to your clients/customers.

In the same way that great chefs ultimately get discovered and become famous (and wealthy), so will you if you focus on your business as a craft instead of focusing on the goal of growth, wealth and fame.

What if you stood up in front of your company and told them you were a business filled with craftspeople? No endless stories about three-year strategic plans and organizational charts. What if those meetings became ways for everyone to share and perfect their craft? To borrow from the chef analogy again, what if everyone was sharing their latest recipe/dish and getting feedback to make it even better?

To me, that sounds like a lot of fun. A business I would love to work IN.

Yes, of course, you need to spend time working ON your business. You will naturally do so because you can't evolve your craft without looking at what else is required to continue to be the best at it.

Want scale? Shift your focus to how to scale your craft versus scaling your business. There is nothing permanently exhilarating about thinking about how to scale your business. How to deliver the highest level of your craft to more people is the problem to enjoy solving.

Not every business can be Apple, Amazon or Google. But every business can be one that delivers its particular craft with joy. Every business can be fun to run.

A Business Filled with Craftspeople

Practicing your craft creates so much value, uniqueness and joy. Imagine if you built a business where everyone was nurtured as a craftsperson in whatever role they had.

Imagine the type of business that would be.

I mean REALLY imagine it.

In order to move towards this dream, the people within your organization will have to rise up to match your vision or move on to a company better suited for them.

When you set this standard for who works at your company, some people will leave or you will have to let some people go.

Other than finances, if there is one thing that causes business owners more stress, time and worry it is managing employees. Specifically, finding and sustaining valued employees that care about their work, the business and its clients. In order to have a business filled with people that care this much, you will have to deal with employees quitting, and having to let employees go.

Regardless of the scenario, replacing someone eats up an enormous amount of time and energy. As always, time is also money. Consider these numbers based on a number of studies done by HR and payroll companies. Take a 50-person company with an average per-employee salary of $68,000. If they lose and hire 10 people each year, the total cost to the business is over $350,000.

How can it be improved?

I do not have all the answers on this. But here are five lessons I have learned over the past 30+ years.

Lesson Number 1: People will leave. Solve for it.

You can read all the books you want about having a great office culture and building a workplace where nobody would ever quit. People will still leave or you will need to let someone go.

When that happens, you need to cover their work and begin the process of finding a replacement. That process, no matter who you are, is a drag. Posting the job, reading resumes, scheduling interviews and getting a new person up to speed can take months. Paying a headhunter is very expensive. Do it a few times a year and much of your year will be stuck in the hiring process.

Why not start with the given that people will leave? Make prospecting for talent as important as prospecting for clients/customers. Where you usually post a job when there is an opening (and, therefore, playing defense instead of offense), try posting for the type of people you would like to add to your business whether you have an opening or not. Literally create a pipeline for hiring prospects and leads in your CRM software or on a spreadsheet you check regularly. Set a goal to have 10 to 15 people that would be a great addition to your business when you have a spot. Schedule to meet three to five new people every month. This approach will pay off in many ways beyond hiring.

Lesson Number 2: Always raise your average.

I got this advice long ago: Every new hire should raise the average of your team. If they do not, you should not make the hire. I know it is tempting to just get someone hired so you can get back to work. Remember, the level of your team will track directly to the level of your business. Therefore, you MUST view each new hire as an opportunity to improve your business.

"Will this person be significantly better than the person they are replacing?" is the only question you need to be asking. If the answer is no, I suggest you deal with the short term pain the job vacancy creates and hold out for someone that will add value to your business. OR, remember Fewer Better. Consider if the job needs to be replaced. Could you hire someone with different skills to match where you want your business to go?

Even if the person leaving was a rockstar employee, still look to raise the average. Something great happens when you can look at someone leaving as an opportunity instead of as a hit to the business.

Lesson Number 3: Do not try to engineer an exit.

Consider two scenarios that may sound familiar:

1 You have someone that is not a great fit for your business but you do not want to fire them. So you stop giving them raises and wait for them to find another job, thinking you will avoid a severance payment and your stress over firing them.

2 Someone threatens to leave unless you give them a big bump in pay. So you give in and pay them and tell yourself you will replace them when it suits you best|.

I have tried both scenarios many times and they never end well. Ultimately, the employee leaves when it's least convenient for you. Or you end up with a letter from an employment lawyer.

If you can "rip off the Band-Aid" with candor and empathy, it will lead to a better result. If you cannot give the employee the increase, then explain it to them. If they have to leave, then let them leave. (See Lesson 1: People will leave.) If they are worth more money, be proactive about rewarding them. If they are not, then you now have an opportunity to raise your average. Let them go with the dignity they deserve and do all you can to help them find a new spot where they can raise the average for someone else. (Another bonus tip: Stay connected to them and prove that your desire to help them was not just words. If they are leaving with integrity, do right by them and it will come back to you tenfold.)

Lesson Number 4: The annual performance review is a relic.

How often do members of your team leave an annual performance review happy with what they heard and the bonus and/or increase you offered? When anything builds up for a year, there can only be a letdown. This does not mean I think you should be giving out increases so often that your payroll gets ahead of your revenue.

Again, I think you need to change the game and stop following cold corporate models. I have found that most people just want to know the path they have at your company, what they can hope to achieve during their time with you, and how it will help them fulfill the dreams they have for their life.

Therefore, your employee reviews should live at the intersection of the biggest dreams you have for the business AND the biggest dreams the employee wants to achieve for themselves.

Stop thinking you need to spend an hour telling someone about all the areas where they are failing and where they are weak. You hated it when your teachers did that in school, and it's not any better as an adult. Drop these relics that were designed for different times.

Instead, make a short list of what your employees are the very best at. Then work with your employees on automating or delegating everything else. No, not tomorrow. If an employee exits a review meeting knowing how they are going to spend more and more time doing what they love and less time struggling against where they are weak, the whole business benefits.

Remember, you are looking for each person to be on their journey to be a craftsperson in whatever role they take on. How can you help them get there?

Lesson Number 5: Your employees are NOT entrepreneurs. Stop expecting them to be okay with your wild ride.

Remember that as an entrepreneur, you are fine not knowing what the future brings and changing direction on a dime. Your employees? Not so much.

I cannot tell you how often I explain this to my clients: Your employees are NOT entrepreneurs. If they were, they would be running their own businesses. Stop expecting them to behave like entrepreneurs or to be comfortable with your "fly by the seat of your pants" approach to running a business. A little empathy for how your entire team thinks and feels will go a long way here.

While you thrive on uncertainty, they thrive on knowing exactly where the business is heading, their specific role in the plan, and how their careers will keep rising all along the way. Without them understanding these specifics, you are leaving yourself open to a competitor coming along and filling the void your employee feels. If you are creating this void in your employees' minds, then do not be so shocked when they come and tell you they took an offer from your competitor.

The current reactionary approach we take to staff disruption is sapping time and energy from our businesses and stressing us out! We feel defeated when someone leaves. We rush the hiring process and we worry about the mood it creates in the business.

Be clear with everyone about how you think about people leaving. Be clear about what you reward the team for. Get ahead of the process so someone leaving feels like an opportunity to improve the business. Keep those that leave - as long as they leave with integrity - in your orbit.

If you are worried about what anyone outside your company thinks about people leaving - competitors that like to gossip and waste their time thinking about you - then remember a line from my first book, *Your Business Brickyard:* "Your competitors do not pay your bills and they NEVER will."

GET YOUR TEAM
TOGETHER. BRING
YOUR CHISELS
AND GET TO
WORK.

The Reverse Michelangelo

Famed artist and sculptor Michelangelo believed that the statues he carved were already inside the blocks of marble. His job as the sculptor was to simply remove the right bits of marble that would set the statue free. It is a lovely image to consider. In my experience, it's the opposite of what happens in most businesses. Maybe even yours.

I want to propose a process that I lovingly call, "The Reverse Michelangelo."

Why?

These past few years, my business transformation work has been less and less about pivoting a business to a new market or altering their marketing and/or sales strategy. Instead, it has been chipping away at all of the excess products, services, staff and related expenses that have been added to the business over the years.

The statue, in this case, is where the business began. A beautiful and focused core idea built on the specific talents of the founder/owner/partners and team. A problem in the market they felt needed to be solved and so they focused on doing exactly that. Some success arrived in the form of a bunch of clients/customers and maybe even, gasp, some profits.

Then somewhere it stopped being *enough.*

Some version of, "Why don't we get into complementary business lines," or, "What if we offered more services that our clients may need or could use," took over. **The popular but damaging idea that growth is about *more of more instead of more of less.***

Every time this happened, a slab of clay obscured the business until what the business was known for and best at was obscured completely. Profits disappeared or were reduced while everyone incorrectly focused on revenue growth.

Recently I worked intensely with a business that had obscured their statue beyond visibility. They decided to follow the examples of tech startups and giant competitors as they hired for growth that matched the scale they someday hoped to achieve. They expanded into business lines that were not their true expertise and, most importantly, not businesses they cared about. Four different companies existed when I arrived, none were profitable. Just a hope that someday, with scale, they would be.

While I am thinking of a specific business as I wrote that last paragraph, I can think of plenty I have worked with that I would describe the same way. Maybe you thought I was talking about yours?

In every case, there was enormous pride in being able to say how big the staff had become, the annual revenue growth and how many services they offered. But, as we've discussed, Fuck Your Pride.

What are you the best at? Why did your clients choose you?

Why are you not doing just that?

Some versions of these questions, answered without ego or pride, will allow you to cut deep into the stone. More often than not, the answers do not reveal a new business to build but the earliest days of the same business. The reason the business came to be in the first place. The role it plays better than any other if you would just let that be enough. If you could see that innovating around what your business does better than anyone else means you will never be done innovating, improving, evolving and growing.

How many activities is your business currently involved in that it is not great at? How many business lines generate the right amount of profit - enough to make it worth the effort and expense? Bonus point question so you keep fueling your passion for the business... How many of those activities do you love doing?

My hunch is that there is a core inside your business (the original sculpture) that is sharing a lot of time, attention and money with products and/or services that other businesses do better than yours.

Why spend your time on those extraneous products and services?

I asked my recent client if he wanted a company with 60+ people in staff that did $20 million in revenue and $300 thousand in profit, or an eight-person company doing $5 million in revenue and $2 million in profit.

You probably just read that and thought the answer was crystal clear. I do not think it is or we would have many more highly focused businesses that stick to their crafts.

Sure, it is great to be able to tell people how fast you are growing revenue and headcount. The problem is when most of that is just marble or stone obscuring the beautiful sculpture that could be your ideal business.

What is the sculpture that WAS once your business? What have you added that is suffocating it - and likely choking you along with it?

Ironically, the more you focus on what your core business actually is the more depth you will find you can offer through it. Focusing on the business you should actually be in creates more time to figure out how to be the best in the world at one thing, not 10.

Get your team together. Bring your chisels and get to work.

My client is now down to a core group of people and will turn a substantial profit this year. Everything else has been outsourced to businesses that do those pieces as their core business. It is a powerful shift in strategy that saved millions of dollars and will generate millions in profit.

It turns out that they are back to the business that they started 10 years ago, brought back to life in a more modern way today. The momentum it has created will allow them to double their profits in 2021... IF they do not allow anything to ever obscure their sculpture again.

> **"**
>
> SAVE YOUR
> "WHY" FOR
> YOUR INTERNAL
> MEETINGS OR YOUR
> COZY OFF-SITES.

Nobody Cares about Your "Why"

> "If you go out there and start making
> noise and making sales - people will find
> you. Sales cure all. You can talk about
> how great your business plan is and how
> well you are going to do. You can make
> up your own opinions, but you cannot
> make up your own facts. Sales cure all."
>
> - DAYMOND JOHN

With my apologies to author Simon Sinek, NOBODY really cares about your "Why."

They want you to care about _THEIRS_.

Almost every business owner I talk to these days has figured out their "Why" (and cannot WAIT to tell me all about it). The problem is that stating and broadcasting their Why has not helped their ability to clearly articulate why someone should actually buy their product or service. Even worse, knowing their Why has not helped them win new clients.

The reason is quite simple.

Nobody cares about your Why. They care about theirs.

If you cannot explain how you will help new clients realize THEIR Why, you will lose new business you could have won.

I know, I know, we've all watched Simon Sinek's TED talk where he explains how Apple uses their "Why" to rule the world. Then we have had tons of meetings to throw away those past mission statements so we could replace them with our awesome shiny new Whys.

If only it was so simple to win the hearts, minds and dollars of the customers and clients we crave.

Back in the real world, your customers buy your product or use your service because they need it.

How effectively you convince them your product fits their Why matters far more to the future of your business than YOUR Why.

Uber and Lyft can talk all they want about their Why to solve transportation for the world.

It doesn't matter. Just think about it... Do you give a shit about their mission?

What matters to you and me is we hit the "I want a car right now" button on our apps, a car shows up and takes us where we want to go. Full stop.

Whoever is the best at doing that reliably, within some pricing constraints, wins.

So let's jump into your next big pitch to a customer or client.

I will bet that your main pitch deck starts off with an "About Us" slide which is followed by 15-20 minutes that is ALL about your business, then a few more slides about your past work, your past clients and then maybe even an org chart to show off your staff. Somewhere in there you explain your purpose, mission or Why.

You, you and you.

Pleasssssssssse... stop.

Before you make another pitch to a client you want to win, just start with this simple question: What is THEIR Why?

What buyers want from you at that moment is to make them ridiculously confident that you can solve THEIR problem and accelerate THEIR mission with the least amount of effort on their part.

The more you are talking about anything else, the less they care. (Side note, if it takes you more than 10 slides to do it all, keep editing.)

When I say you will solve their problem, I am talking about solving it allllll the way until the results show up in THEIR bank account.

Fuck your pride. Nobody really cares how the sausage is made, they just care how it tastes and how it fixes their hunger.

If I could design the perfect pitch meeting, I would walk into the room, have no slides on a wall, and simply state the following:

"NOBODY is better at [Insert whatever it is that you do best] so that you can [Insert the measurable benefit they will realize and how it accelerates their Why]."

Then I would drop a fat printed book filled with 100 past customers/clients attesting to how you rocked their world and are worth 20 times whatever you charge.

I would then field as many questions as they have about how they can get started working with you, the costs and how much time you need to deliver the 20 times results you promised.

Drop the mic and walk out. You've won.

The challenge for you is how perfectly you can complete the blanks in the opening statement about what you do best and the specific results they will see in their bank account.

Not in that cold corporate jargon that only serves to make you feel good about yourself, but in plain English so anyone will understand how powerful it will be for them and THEIR mission.

If you are not the best at whatever niche you are looking to sell to, you now know what you have to get to work on.

If you cannot clearly articulate how your ideal client will realize a measurable benefit that is a large multiple of your fees then you need to figure it out. NOW.

Save your "Why" for your internal meetings or your cozy offsites.

Instead, just follow these three steps:

1. Understand what your business is the best at doing (and who would value it the most).

2. Know precisely how your customers/clients realize INSANE value from it (and how you will make it happen with the least amount of effort on their part).

3. Be relentless about building momentum around 1 and 2.

WHERE'S MY STUFF? SIMPLE AND CLEAR. AND WHAT OUR CLIENTS VALUED THE MOST.

Where's My Stuff?

> "*There are not more than five musical notes, yet the combinations of these five give rise to more melodies than can ever be heard. There are not more than five primary colors, yet in combination they produce more hues than can ever been seen.*"
>
> - SUN TZU, *THE ART OF WAR*

My logistics company was acquired by a large global competitor in 2000. The acquiring company also bought a number of our competitors right around the same time. Our new corporate overlords thought it would be a good idea to bring us, now former business owners, all together to talk about ways we could work, integrate, create synergies and a whole variety of other big business buzzwords.

As we "geniuses" sat around the large boardroom table, we talked about slick new ideas to link our computer systems, innovative marketing ideas and the like.

I was in full "blue sky" mode.

After 15 minutes, someone finally piped in and said, "That all sounds great gang, but when clients call me the only thing they give a shit about is: *Where's my stuff?*"

He was right and I was SO wrong.

In the cargo/shipping business, "Where's my stuff?" is what MATTERS the most to our clients. Everything else we do may be important to the process but, when valuable cargo is traveling across the globe, removing the unknown can make it as stress-free as delivering it across town. If you could be the very best at keeping your clients in the know about the whereabouts of their "stuff," then you would be alone at the top of the industry.

I speak and write a lot about the need for a company to think bigger and simultaneously focus on their basics.

Most people decide that they must go away and come up with something so complicated that it will be impossible for their competitors to compete. They feel that if it is too simple then their business is not sexy or unique enough. They are wrong.

Restaurants need to create food that tastes amazing. If the food is lousy, it does not matter how nice the place looks or how great the service is.

Airlines need to get you safely from point A to point B on time and at the lowest cost. In-plane TV, Wi-Fi and fancy airport terminals matter little if you can't get to your destination.

I could go on and on (and often do). Every business in every industry has their basic. The businesses that dominate their industry know their basic and stay relentlessly focused on doing everything they can to prove it. It fuels their innovation, marketing and the reason their company exists. It stops them from having meetings (and wasting time, energy and money) to talk about anything that does not help them deliver that basic with perfection.

Where's my stuff? Simple and clear. And what our clients valued the most.

Do you know the equivalent of "Where's my stuff?" for your clients? How well do you solve for it? How well do you communicate and prove it?

SECTION TWO

CHANGE YOUR PACE

STOP WITH
THE HUSTLE
AND GRIND
BULLSHIT.

Go Slow to Go Fast

I never thought that I had any aerobic capacity. I have worked out with weights for years but had become convinced that I had smaller lungs or some other lie I told myself enough to believe it as truth.

A few years ago, I decided to follow my own *Fuck Your Pride* advice and start running.

For myself.

At first, the goal was to run one mile. This may seem like a simple goal but it was not easy for me.

I now can run a 10K with relative ease and am targeting a half marathon in the coming months.

What I want to share with you is how my initial approach to running was all wrong. For the first six months, I pushed myself to run as hard and fast as possible. Each time, I finished gasping for air and with legs that were wrecked for the next few days. But grinding as hard as you can and going as quickly as you can is what it is all about. Right? No pain, no gain, etc.

About five months into my endeavor, I stumbled upon a great book called *Finding Ultra* by one of my favorite podcasters, Rich

Roll. This very well written book is about a lot more than running. Mr. Roll takes up running after a long battle with alcoholism. His goal, at first, was just to get healthy for his family and himself. As he progresses, he decides he needs a more audacious goal and sets his sights on running a race called the Ultraman. The Ultraman entails swimming 6.2 miles, cycling 260 miles and running 52.4 miles over three consecutive days.

To accomplish this, Rich (yes, I am calling Rich by his first name with the hope that he will read this and instantly want to hang out) searches for a coach to help him prepare to finish this extreme race in just a few months.

When he reached out to ultra-endurance coach Chris Hauth, Rich was already running 20+ miles at a time in the hills and mountains near Los Angeles. What his new coach told him caught him by complete surprise.

"You need to slow down if you want to go fast."

It turns out that the old idea of running with your heart rate chugging along at your aerobic capacity just burns out your muscles and is not nearly as efficient in building the long-term aerobic foundation you need for longer distances. (Heart rate is measured in beats per minute, or BPM. Your aerobic capacity is roughly 220 minus your age. For me that's 170 beats per minute.)

The better approach is heart zone training which is MUCH slower than you are probably used to at first. For me, it means staying in the 140 BPM range. I can go as fast as possible, as long as I keep my heart rate in that zone. This zone allows me to enjoy my runs and go for much longer distances. At first, it felt more like a fast walk than a run, but fairly quickly I sped up while keeping my heart rate in this lower zone. More importantly, I was able to run daily without the soreness and fatigue that had made running so difficult for me to sustain in the past. My distances quickly increased.

My resting heart rate improved. I had built a foundation and a lasting capacity to go faster and farther. By going slower.

The same rule applies to business.

Stop with the hustle and grind bullshit. Slow down and spend the time on the fewer better things that will create a foundation of incredible speed and capacity in your business.

Most businesses are stuck racing to only realize incremental gains. They do not take the time to think bigger and then take even more time to build up the capacity required to realize the leaps in growth they truly want but lack the patience to obtain.

If every year you are racing to hit your numbers and hope the next year will be a bit better, then you must change the way you think about your pacing.

You know the saying, it's a marathon and not a sprint? It makes us feel good to say it. How often do we live it?

GO SLOW TO GO FAST.

> **"**
> FEWER SHORT-
> TERM ANXIETIES
> MEAN BETTER
> LONG TERM
> RESULTS.

Your 36-Month Year

A traveling salesman is walking down a country road when he sees something that stops him dead in his tracks. There, under an apple tree, a farmer is straining to lift a heavy pig so it can eat an apple out of the tree. When the pig is finished with one apple, the farmer shuffles over to the next apple and the pig keeps chomping. After watching this for 15 minutes, the traveling salesman cannot control himself and shouts out to the farmer, "Hey! wouldn't it save a lot of time if you just knocked a bunch of apples out of the tree and let the pig eat them off of the ground?" The farmer looks back at the salesman, puzzled, and says, "What does time matter to a pig?"

How would you run your business if you landed on a new planet and their year was 36 months long instead of 12? Where, like the pig, you ran your business at your own pace.

While you consider that question, let me explain why I am asking...

Right now, you are thinking about the end of your month, your quarter or your year. You are likely in a mad dash to make or break your numbers from this same time last year and your targets for the full year. You push on your team members, you push on your clients, you pressure your prospects and you make deals to attain a "score" you set in January.

This is how it goes every year, over and over. Sprint after sprint. Quarter to quarter and then year after year, while never feeling like you can do the things that would create the size and scale of the business you truly want. All because of a calendar construct you did not create.

Each year ends with all kinds of crafty decisions about pushing expenses off to next year, giving special deals to prospects so they sign in this calendar year, while you steal revenue from your next year. It is a ridiculous dance we never seem to stop.

Why?

We hear admired public companies announce their quarterly numbers and we see their stock rise and fall based on how they did and how they say they will do. So we measure ourselves the same way in our businesses.

Why?

If you are not a public company and do not have shareholders that are measuring your quarterly or annual performance, then why does it matter? Seriously. As long as your profit margins are healthy and cash flow is strong then why do you care so much about the short term?

Sure, there are annual employee increases to manage and taxes to pay based on a 12-month year. But you can change how you reward your team based on the long term goals that matter to you most. If you are communicating well, those goals should matter equally to your team.

You can simply treat taxes as three known expenses across your 36-month year.

So, imagine now that I roll out a new year for you. A year that is 36 months long. You now have 36 months to build a business that will finally be what you really want at the end of this new, MUCH longer, year. No arbitrary sprints. Just the right amount of time to build something that will make you proud.

Anything is possible for your business in 36 months. The secret is finally allowing yourself the time and space to execute a plan worthy of a 36-month year (Remember, go slow to go fast).

In the early months, you can "plant seeds in new fields" and build up the machine that will be able to produce massive results.

- A 36-month year allows for patience.

- A 36-month year allows everyone in the company to be aligned with your long term goals.

- A 36-month year eases the pressure that you deal with every single year.

Whether you want to sell your business, double revenue, transform into new markets, or just double your profit, you need to create as long a year as you need to make the smartest moves to get there.

Let patience be your business virtue.

As Leo Tolstoy said, "The two most powerful warriors are patience and time."

So how do you start to put this new mindset into practice?

I want you to go get your current annual budget and then add two more years to the right of the annual totals for this year. Just one column for each year after this one will suffice.

Starting 36 months from now, think about where you want your business to be if you are no longer worried about the next quarter or the next year. How much revenue, from what type of offerings? How and where will you want to refine, grow and evolve? Who will you need to hire? What type of changes need to be made to your infrastructure? What will it all cost?

First, fill in the rough revenue and expense items for two years.

Then work backwards and fill out where you need to be 12 months before that, so you are on pace to hit the end of your 36-month year.

If you do this honestly, you should find that where you are pushing towards is way too focused on winning this year instead of winning the larger future you really want, a future that has likely eluded you for too many years.

Now, and only now, rethink your current year budget to start to reflect your long term plans.

Sit with the spreadsheet for a few weeks. It will be natural for your 36-month goal to be infected by your 12-month thinking.

Changing years of quarterly and yearly thinking will take some time.

Just allow yourself to **really** imagine what you could do if you just had more time to create lasting change.

Remember, a 12-month year is playing someone else's game. It causes persistent short-term decision-making that is hurting the long term results of your business and the exponential growth and results you truly want. **Fewer short-term anxieties mean better long term results.**

The first day of the next month is the start of YOUR 36-month year.

Start playing YOUR game.

START BY
RECOGNIZING WHAT
YOUR BUSINESS
ACTUALLY FEELS
LIKE TO YOU TODAY.

The Bumpy Plateau

When people talk about the life cycle of a business, they typically draw a simple bell curve. A steady rise that ultimately leads to a moment where it all begins to fall. (Yes, make it over a long enough period and they all drop.) But that moment isn't a moment at all. Preceding that descent, the business had entered a period of many years that I call "the bumpy plateau."

Every business starts off with passion and purpose. Deals are made on the fly, systems are cobbled together as needed, and the can-do attitude is limitless. As the business scales, it keeps structures loose and grows by simply adding bodies to keep up with new business (add a client, add an employee, etc.) After a certain time, the structure that has worked for so long can only sustain a certain volume of business and so it levels out to a plateau.

Here is where so much of the frustration begins. This is when the passion starts to bleed away because you begin to spend most of your time *in* your business instead of *on* it. This is when you deal with increasing customer complaints, staffing issues, cash flow hiccups, and so on. What is tricky about the plateau is that it never feels flat. You push ahead with a new sales focus and start to land a few new clients, but then you lose a few because the structure of the business cannot support the growth. Business grows organically in good economic times and then falls as the economy naturally dips. So you ride and fight along that plateau for months and years, growing a little and slipping back. Bouncing along until this existence becomes all you can remember about what it is like to run your business. The fun drifts away and a grind is all that is left.

Most business owners are blind to the problem. It is like the frog, coming gently to boil, that never jumps out of the pot. (See Section Five: Risk and Resilience.) The bumpy plateau does not feel painful. But it is frustrating. You feel close to growing again and yet you never do. Like a big tease, the next level of your business remains just out of reach. So you keep at it. You bring in a marketing company, you change your branding, and you hire the salesperson who will change your future. They all fail.

"So, I must not know what I am doing anymore," you think as you drive home after another stressful day. "I have lost my touch. This doesn't feel like it used to. Why do I feel like we are not getting anywhere when I am working so hard?"

What to do?

Let's get tactical:

1 Get back to Fewer Better. Figure out what your business does better than any other. Cut away all of the bloat and complexity that has piled up over the years. Don't expect it to all get resolved quickly. Map out everything that needs to get done, prioritize it, and get started. Read my book, *Your Business Brickyard,* which is all about just this.

2   See your business from the outside in. As I say in *Your Business Brickyard,* "It is hard to read the label from inside the bottle." That is a human frailty and not an organizational one. When I begin to work with a client, most of my job is to simply be a mirror. To listen carefully to everything that is going on and then show them the picture they just painted for me. They are shocked every time. They know the dysfunctional picture to be true and yet they never see it themselves. The same happens to me with my business. Often. Congrats, you are human.

Then what?

Re-imagine.

You need to redesign your business based on what you want it to be. For a simple example, let's say you want to grow your business from $10 million in sales to $40 million in the next five years. The company structure that properly manages $10 million simply cannot support a company that is properly managing $40 million. But there is a structure that can and you have to design it. You have to architect, in as much detail as possible, what your company looks like when it is managing $40 million in sales. Don't just plan what it looks like at twice the size, because that just has you adding people to do more of the same. That is the process that keeps you on the plateau. Instead, envision the businesses you are in at that future state. How many clients do you have? How many people do you need to keep them happy, and what type of new people did you need to bring in to get you there? What technology is powering it all? What infrastructure will you need?

Notice how different this structure, created from a blank canvas, differs from the business you are running today. Once you have painted that picture, then your work becomes clear on how to create the path from where you are today to where you want to be. Now you can tell your marketing/PR/design firm exactly what you need them to do. You can inspire your entire company with the new hill you want to conquer together. You are no longer thinking about the type of company you wish you had. You now have a roadmap to build the company you truly desire.

Get back to start-up mode.

We often imagine a start-up to be three people in a small room or garage getting ready to take the world by storm. But who says that is what a start-up needs to be? Some business owners may chuckle because they think a big company cannot possibly act like a start-up. Why not? Being a start-up is as much a mindset as anything else. It's about making decisions without endless meetings and deliberations. Where you execute relentlessly because you want to win each and every new client.

Reconnect to what it felt like when you were starting out. Bring everyone along with you since they will have forgotten as well. Figure out what parts of your day must be automated or delegated so you can spend more days like you used to.

Again, there is a lot of hard work to do and there is no guarantee of success. Sure, the economic environment, your competition, or bad luck may work against you. But all of that would be true along that plateau as well.

We have traits that help us create great success and we have traits that hold us back. Welcome to the club. But you always get to decide where you go from here.

I challenge you to go find your smile again. Start by recognizing what your business actually feels like to you today. Then be determined to change it.

PROFIT

REVENUE IS AN
EGO METRIC.
PROFIT IS A
FREEDOM METRIC.

Profit Is Your Freedom Metric

There are two (not twenty two) areas that create the outcome that will solve every other goal, dream, purpose and possibility for your business. And they both have to do with PROFIT.

Here is the focused profit multiplier approach I use with my clients:

1 Determine the cost to reliably <u>attract and sign</u> the maximum new clients/customers in the shortest time.

The key word here is *reliably*. Do you have a rock-solid, repeatable process to connect with your prospects, make them an irresistible offer and have them sign on the dotted line?

I am talking about being totally dialed in on your ideal customers and having a way to reach their eyes, ears, minds and hearts. Not a new website, logo or brochure. Not just random social media activity. Not salespeople that are prospecting and hoping to hit quotas. A real start-to-finish system, based in the world we live in today (not how it was done 10, 15 or 20 years ago), that you know will generate a steady flow of new business every month, quarter and year.

A full system, not just sales calls. A process and not merely activity. Scalable and not based on just setting higher goals. R E L I A B L E.

Is this system as efficient as it can be so that the cost of gaining a new customer/client is always moving lower? Are you continually reducing the time it takes to sign a new customer/client? Side note: Do you know your current cost of acquiring a customer and how long it takes from start to finish?

This means you stop poo-pooing (yes, I said it... and I even looked up the spelling) sales and marketing ideas that nobody has done in your industry or that seem foreign (or scary) to you. "That will never work in my industry," is a phrase you need to lose forever. The goal here is to do what must be done until you know exactly how you will bring in X clients this month, quarter and year. To have total control over how that will happen.

Now think how that will shift your enjoyment of your business. What it will do to your confidence as you start work each day? How it will change your life and those that fight alongside you?

2 Continually optimize the cost to <u>retain and delight</u> your clients/customers.

Here is the part that is far from sexy and requires some hard choices. This is where you must stop and understand your payroll at a deeper level, along with every expense in the business. What percentage of your payroll is focused on delivering above the expectations you set out in your sales process? How are you creating moments of delight so your clients never leave and eagerly refer you to others? Every expense not connected to this should be looked at for elimination. That includes employees.

Figuring out your people, your expenses and making them match ONLY what you need to retain and delight your clients/customers is a full-time job. Few do it well.

Too many are stuck on org charts, titles and who reports to whom. Instead, everyone in the company should either be attracting and signing customers/clients or retaining and delighting them. Period. I have yet to read an organizational chart that is structured around these two, and only these two, areas of focus. Is yours? You will find that every function of your business will fit nicely into this structure.

But, you say, profit does not matter for me. I am focused on growing revenue and the profit will follow. "Our goal is to be at $X million in revenue by 2025." I used to believe the same. But I ran a business with a ton of revenue and very little profit based on the idea that scale would lead to higher profit margins *someday*. That day is elusive. All those one-time expenses that stole profit this year turn out to be the type of expenses that somehow show up every year. Crises come up so you have to hire faster or for more money than you should. The drive for revenue growth without equal or greater focus on net profit creates bloat that is messy, if not near impossible, to correct.

Please do not tell me about Amazon and the decades of losses they had for the sake of revenue growth. If you think your private business is anything like Amazon, then this is clearly not the approach for you.

For the rest of you hung up on revenue as your key metric, remember this:

Revenue is an ego metric.

Profit is a freedom metric.

Profit will fuel the freedom you crave. You will find that profit is what makes your business thrive and deliver on its mission. Profit enables your business to give back in any way that fulfills you. But wait, there's more... It will also pay for the mortgage, your vacations, school for your kids, and allow you to do great things for those you care about, plus fill your savings, rainy day, and retirement accounts.

Consider how you would spend your time if you were only focused on perfecting this formula in your business. The creativity and fun you could bring to it all. Yes, you would be focused on *fewer*, but there is so much *better* to do within this streamlined approach.

Let's begin!

Profit Matters

I cannot tell you how many businesses I have worked with that had profit margins well below 10%. (Profit margins are the amount that your total revenue exceeds your total costs.) Many would tell me that low margin percentage was typical for the industry.

No matter what, low margins put your company at significant risk. Live with them at your peril.

I am 54. I have lived and worked through two "once-in-a-life-time" recessions (and one global pandemic) in just the last 25 years. I likely will go through a few more, as will you. Recessions are not the only risk business owners face. A large client could leave or a new competitor could impact pricing and sales.

When your profit margin is low, any shock to the business will drop your business below "sea level" and into losses. Once there, you will be forced to be reactive, start shedding expenses and pushing too hard to get new business at any cost. It is a death spiral. Sometimes slow and sometimes fast. I have lived it myself and I have met clients enduring it. There is nothing fun about it and it can make you live under extreme stress for years. I hope to convince you to take bold steps to avoid it, NOW.

When a business operates at a 20-25% profit margin, sure, a shock to the system will hurt. Maybe it even drops margins down to 10%. But, at those levels, you are surviving while your competitors are below water. You have the money to be patient. You do not have to change your 36-month year plan. Your business is not at risk. You are in position to go on offense during difficult times.

Regardless of your industry, you can get there. Here are just two tactics to try out:

1   **Reset Your Budget:** Take your current revenue and write down 75% of that number. How could you alter your expenses so that they are no more than your current revenue? If you are at 25% already, then work against 65% of your revenue. You are not doing this to be greedy or harsh. This is about removing risk from your business.

Get real with yourself here. What expenses are not necessary to do what matters the most to your clients? (What THEY care about, not what you think they care about.) Where are you spending money just because it was "in the budget" for this year? You know, the budget that was constructed to operate at a 8-10% margin. What would your budget look like if you decided you must operate at two to three times that profit margin?

Once you set it, this is the margin you commit to maintain. Explain to everyone in the business that you are doing it to protect the business and everyone who cares about it. I have a client that takes any profit higher than their 20% target and puts it into a bonus pool. Everyone understands why the budget was reset and that it was not about the owner just wanting to make more money for themselves. The personal income of *everyone* in the business has grown as a result.

2 **Innovative Pricing/Fees:** How do you charge for your product or service? If your industry operates at 8-10% margins, is there a way to change the game and operate at double that? Ask any industry that has been disrupted by online services if they wish they had done it first. Car services, hotels, print media and anyone in retail. There isn't an industry that cannot be disrupted in some way. So, I ask, why not you? Other than your fear, what is stopping you from changing the norm?

This is a chance to create a self-serve offering that could be half the price of your competitors and cost you a fraction to retain and delight your customers/clients. Fewer. Better.

This is a chance to redesign the way you price to better match the way your client's business operates, or to show them you are committed and confident in the results you will deliver.

If you set your pricing like all of your competitors, then you have a chance to change the game. As a personal example, when my clients and I agree on a profit growth metric for them to reach, I put up to 50% of my fee against it. This changes the conversation and works well for me and my clients.

"This is how it has always been done" is just an early draft of a business obituary.

Remember, profit equals freedom for you and your business. Growing it will create innovation, strength and opportunity for everyone that relies on it.

PROFIT LEAPS
ONLY OCCUR IN
AN ENVIRONMENT
THAT DEMANDS
THEM.

Profit Leaps

"When everyone in my firm gets a bonus between $3 and $5 million this year, how am I going to keep them motivated?"

This was the question asked by a hedge fund founder 20+ years ago in a YPO (The Young Presidents Organization - I know, it sounds silly but it is an amazing global organization) group I belonged to. I have never forgotten it. Not just because of the sheer out-of-touchness (not a term but should be) of this being his biggest worry (he was a bit of an ass). But because I was jealous that this arrogant ass was making such a massive profit at the end of the year, and I was not.

Here I was toiling away in my business and, despite the usual bump in growth every year, bonuses were in the tens of thousands of dollars.

For almost every business owner I have met and worked with, this is a similar experience for them as well.

The business grows its revenue at 10, 20, or even 40% each

year. But the annual change in personal income is not life- or lifestyle-altering.

I remembered this story as I was considering the question: What does a business owner really want?

A friend of mine had urged me to dig deep and make a detailed client avatar of my ideal client. You may know the drill: give it a name, a lifestyle, 2.2 kids, etc., and detail out their true wants and desires for their lives and careers.

As I sat there thinking through every client I have had over the years, I kept coming back to a simple answer: They all wanted a lot more money in their personal bank account. The type of real wealth that was created every year from their business. The type of wealth that would allow them to create a true retirement cushion. The type of annual income that would make it easy for their kids to go to the school of their choice. The type of annual bonus that would allow them to easily buy a larger home or go on amazing vacations. The type of wealth that would allow them to give back in whatever way they desired. The lack of large jumps in their income was a festering frustration for them all.

Amidst all the talk about being passionate about our work, having a vision and our businesses having a mission/purpose, this is what I kept coming back to. When a client hires me, ultimately they want their business to grow significantly enough so they can personally make a lot more money. This requires a growth in profit that serves the business growth plans as well.

Sure, business owners want less stress, more fun and to not have to worry about how they are going to pay their mortgage.

But, I asked myself, what ultimately is a cure for a lot of the stress and worry? In the immortal words of ABBA (yes, that ABBA - don't judge me): Money, money, money.

Your new mantra: Profit leaps only occur in an environment that demands them.

We all know that owning a business is fraught with risk. Somewhere we seem to have given a pass to demanding a fat reward that makes the risk really worth it.

The business romantic in me (I know, awwww… So cute!) would prefer my answer had been to make the world a better place. To make a dent in the universe, etc. But when my clients are the most honest with me, they want to make a lot of money so they can enjoy their lives. Then they can use that wealth to make their dent.

So what is causing this cycle of growth without commensurate increases in wealth?

For most businesses, revenue growth is matched closely by expense growth. You get a bunch of clients, you hire a bunch of people. You grow enough to have to invest in IT or a larger office. Each year there is some extraordinary expense that sucks up potential profit growth.

In some cases, the entrepreneur's salary has grown enough so they get a larger house or maybe a vacation home. So now their personal expenses have also grown along with their income. At the end of the day, their business is actually preventing them from achieving the leaps in wealth and security that they truly desire.

Why?

They have not drawn a line in the sand about the profit levels they are committed to creating.

I grew up watching all the Wall Street financial guys drive by in their fancy cars and $3,000 suits. They lived in enormous apartments and had giant vacation homes.

This level of wealth is not created from a $50,000 or $150,000 annual bonus. Their wealth (not including the trust fund kids') was created from operating a business where a $2, $5 or $20 million annual bonus was the norm.

Go ask an investment banker if they will help you sell your business for $3 million and you will get some version of this answer: "We only focus on deal sizes of $50 million or higher because it takes, roughly, the same amount of work to close a $50 million deal as it takes to close a $5 million deal." M&A lawyers will tell you the same story about the amount of paperwork it takes to close a $1 billion deal as a $1 million deal.

It also requires, roughly, the same amount of staff, office expenses, etc.

Somewhere along the way, these bankers and lawyers decided that they were going to draw the line in the sand and leverage their time on deals and clients that would maximize their wealth.

Now, I hear you, an agency, service or product business is not the same as a hedge fund or investment banking business.

Or is it?

Remember, profit leaps only occur in an environment that demands them.

I am willing to bet that there is a competitor in your market that is making an extraordinary amount of profit and that the owner of that business is making 10 times your personal income. I do not care if it is a laundromat chain, a digital agency, a real estate business or a fitness franchise.

Maybe you chalk their success up to their connections, or just dumb luck. Maybe you think they are more talented or smarter than you. Speaking for myself, I have had plenty of competitors that were far from the sharpest knives in the drawer. However, they were smart enough to hire great talent that they could leverage into leaps in profit.

If you can stop rationalizing long enough to take a closer look (fuck your pride), you will see they made a choice that "getting by" each year was not going to be enough.

I am not suggesting that you change your 20% projected growth to 2,000%. I am, however, suggesting that you think about what it would take for your profit to not just grow in small steps, but to LEAP.

What would have to happen in your business for your net profit to quadruple while your expenses stayed roughly the same?

Yes, quadruple. Sit with the idea for a while before you reject it.

A 4X leap in NET PROFIT

AND

A (near) zero increase in expenses

What would have to happen?

If you increase your pricing 4 times, then what would you have to deliver to make that happen? What would you need to offer clients? Who would you need to hire (or acquire)?

How could you deliver results to your clients that were 4 times what they are today? How could you handle 4 times the number of clients you do today with, roughly, the same staff/overhead?

Here comes that mantra: Profit leaps only occur in an environment that demands them.

That means a shift in how you think about how much **profit** you MUST earn and how to constrain the expenses required to create that growth. Remember, revenue is just a metric for your ego.

You see, it is not just my clients that want to make these leaps. I feel the same about my business. For me, I answered that question by figuring out how I can take 20 times as many clients through my process in a year. It allowed me to lower my cost to clients by delivering results in 20% of the time. It's a version of Fewer Better: Lower costs, faster results.

But first, I needed to decide that incremental growth was no longer acceptable to me.

Those Wall Street bankers have a secret that you cannot replicate. Their industries, competitors or markets have long ago baked in what type of wealth creation is expected. More importantly, they have a non-negotiable floor for the amount of money they expect to earn from every transaction, deal and/or client.

So I ask you the same question I ask my clients: **"Why not you?"**

BUSINESS
SHOULD BE
FUN TO RUN!

Spend Less

> "Do what everyone else is doing, but
> spend less money doing it. Or do
> something no one else can do"
>
> - MICHAEL PORTER

This is one of the core accepted definitions of business strategy. The business world is obsessed with the "do something no else can do" part of it. Endless books, consultancies and keynote talks will help you find your "blue ocean." Stumbling on something that nobody else is doing is sexy. It makes us feel unique and cutting edge. Entrepreneurial bragging rights. For most of us, it is very hard to find and too fraught with risk to offer something truly unique. So we keep reading books, hiring innovation agencies and hunting everywhere for secret sauce.

What if you stop and consider that doing "what everyone else is doing, but spending less money doing it" is just as sexy an option? I know, it makes you feel like you are cheap, your competitors will label you the bottom of the market and your pride cannot handle it. Get over it.

Entrepreneurs and CEOs who engineer a business that delivers the same product at a lower price are the ones who win. The trick is how do you do this without lowering your margin or weakening your product. Solving that is just as innovative as reinventing your industry.

Keeping your office rent low, not spending on expensive furniture, controlling every single expense are part of an innovative strategy. Removing time- and money-wasting steps out of every action your organization takes is innovation. Winning more sales with the same (or better) margins than your competitors is just as sweet.

You do not need an innovation consultant or a three-day off-site to get started. You need to lock yourself in a room with your CFO and a ledger with every single expense of last year. Ask hard questions about each one. Does it add to what you do? **Does it make your business better, or does it just make you feel better about your business?** What do we actually need to be spending money on that has a direct connection to what we deliver to our clients? Everything else needs a hard look and, most likely, a hard decision quickly after it.

Expense innovation is not a "thing." It should be for everyone. In the meantime, it can be YOUR secret sauce.

Business should be fun to run!

66

REMOVING TIME- AND
MONEY-WASTING
STEPS OUT OF
EVERY ACTION YOUR
ORGANIZATION TAKES
IS INNOVATION.

SALES & MARKETING

"

HE DELIVERED A
MESSAGE THAT WAS
CONCISE, VALUABLE
AND TOTALLY
RELEVANT.

Panhandler
Marketing Lesson

Panhandlers. Beggars. People who spend their days asking the age old question, "Brother, can you spare a dime?" Cities big and small have them, and their approach is always the same... "Excuse the interruption. I lost my job, have no place to live, have no food, have eight kids and need any money you can spare."

They work the corners and the ATM machines. On the subway, they move from the front car all the way to the back, telling the same story over and over. They follow the exact same formula as their voices drone without emotion. It has become so commonplace that people don't look up or even blink at some of the saddest stories you can imagine.

But one day, I was riding the Q train when a panhandler stood up and announced:

"The next stop is the 14th Street Station. Connections can be made to the X, Y, Z trains. Up on the street you will find Barnes & Noble, Staples, Starbucks and Whole Foods. Please be sure to pick up any newspapers you have left behind to help keep our subway system clean. Thank you and have a nice day."

Passengers smiled, totally focused on him and engaged by him. He delivered a message that was concise, valuable and totally relevant.

He did it with passion and a dose of fun.

His delighted audience paid him generously for it, dropping cash in the bucket he held as they exited the train.

Now, look at your marketing.

Are you simply "shaking a cup of change" at those you hope will pay you or are you delivering information that is truly relevant and valuable to them? Have you allowed some fun and creativity into the mix so your marketing creates something different than what your prospects have come to expect from everyone else in your industry?

Will you not stop experimenting until you find a pitch that makes them smile?

Your Winning Sales Conversation

What if you threw out everything you currently use for sales and marketing? I am talking about a totally blank slate. Freed from all the ways you have been selling and trying to get noticed. What if you threw out every proposal, RFP template and your library of presentation decks?

If you think I am asking because I just want you to simply create better ones, you would be wrong. I bet you have updated them at different times over the years and those incremental updates only created incremental results.

Just because we are doing a lot of activities that look like sales and marketing, doesn't mean we are achieving much of either. We have full pipelines and are excited about being invited to pitch but we are not winning often enough to change the future of our businesses.

But potential dream clients keep inviting us to come and dance for them, and we willingly show up and proudly display our tail feathers. This cycle never plays to our strengths but we persist in repeating the same cycle. Why?

If we can forget about our pride for a moment, how many of these pitches are you actually winning? How many were decided long before you even showed up to pitch? (You do know there is always one bidder who has the relationship locked up before the process even starts...)

It's important to be more mercenary here. The goal of sales and marketing activity is to WIN new business. By winning, I mean they sign on the line that is dotted and their first check is in the bank. The top of the funnel is important. But it will forever be an expense without enough corresponding revenue if you do not figure out how to reliably win better clients.

If you are nodding your head, then why not try a different approach that could reduce wasted energy and set yourself up to consistently win?

What you really want is to have a specific conversation with a prospect that always sets you up to win.

So, what is that ideal conversation for YOU?

No, not storytelling or your brand story. A conversation. A back and forth. You are sharing your knowledge and enlightening your prospect to new ways of looking at their business. Presenting a fresh approach that will yield exponential results. You must want to hear their answers and their point of view. You must want them to challenge you.

"Conversation isn't about proving a point; true conversation is about going on a journey with the people you are speaking with."

– RICKY MAYE

Think back to a golden sales moment in your past when the discussion played right to your strengths. Where the conversation was not about persuasion but instead about what drives you and your business. Where you were talking about the way you wish your industry would see the world.

The discussion that you wish every business was having when they are searching for the product or service that you sell.

Great conversations are memorable. They inspire. They motivate. They connect people together.

Now, with a tireless amount of detail (even if that means that you write it out like a movie script), I urge you to write that conversation down. From the "hello" all the way to "you can make the check out to…"

Your one and only goal for sales going forward is to have this conversation as often as possible. Understanding what that conversation is will change how you sell and, critically, to whom you are selling. Not everyone will want to have this conversation with you. That's great; they just saved you a lot of time.

When you find yourself in these conversations, your proposals will turn into manifestos. Your pitch decks become a catalyst for discussion. Your capabilities and your expertise will come out naturally as part of your winning conversation.

But first, you have to put in the work to really understand the conversations you should be having. This is what sales will mean to you now.

Yes, I know that the common wisdom is to try and figure out what your ideal prospects want and talk about that. The problem is, you do not really know because, in truth, they don't really know.

The surface problem that people name is rarely the real problem. At least not the problem that, if solved, will create the biggest impact. The magic appears when you dig down and uncover the big issue where you can change the game for your prospect. The right conversation will lead to this transformative moment.

"But Howard," you say, "I get the shift, but what do I do to have these conversations all the time?"

You focus your marketing solely on seeding ideas that work as catalysts to your winning conversation. No more marketing to make noise (I am looking at you, social media). Fewer soundbytes, better conversations.

Consider how you would trigger a conversation at a party or just with a close friend. Not a "How's the weather?" superficial type of conversation. I am talking about a layered and thought-provoking conversation. Damn near an intervention.

If you want to get to this level, you need to challenge people with questions that are not so easily answered or ignored. Questions that point to a solution that would be game-changing if realized. Questions that spark imagination and create intrigue. Questions that will save them money and time. Questions that will make them money or increase their status.

Questions that feel like you are teaching and enlightening. Not selling.

How would your sales process feel if your only goal was simply inviting interested people to meet and talk about it?

1   What are those questions for you? Write them ALL down. Refine and iterate until they are impossible to ignore. (Do not play it safe here. Safe is forgettable. Agitate!)

2   What conversations should each question trigger? Describe them. (You can write many scripts.)

3   Who do you most want to have those conversations with? Make a specific list. Industry, titles, and the people you may already know.

You can always rejoin the herd and write proposals and be part of a bid process when you are done trying a different approach. If you start thinking about creating great conversations, you may find your pitch decks and proposals will be forever changed as a result. So I ask you again, what are the right conversations for your business to be in? How will you create more of them?

GETTING A "BLACK
BELT" IN GROWTH
HACKING WOULD
SERVE YOUR
BUSINESS WELL.

Reliably Attracting New Business

Now that we have started to focus on getting our profit margins to the right levels, marketing messages that surprise and a better sales conversation, let's discuss how you reliably attract the right business.

Above everything else, shining a critical light on how you currently market and sell will make the biggest shift for you. If you're like most of the businesses I've met and work with, you have salespeople, brochures, a nice website, the pricing structure that you've used for the last 15 years and the acknowledgement that you will sell to anyone that is willing to buy from you.

Maybe you still even cold call, or perhaps you send email campaigns. Maybe you dabble a bit on social media, or do a bit of all of it. The key aspect here is that while some of this may work some of the time, it is not RELIABLE. What you MUST have is a fully running system to bring in new business that you can rely on.

I urge you to build a self-running system, a system that is managed as a process from start to finish. The best example I have found is the world of growth hacking.

Growth hackers on the Web have figured out the science and the systems to understand customers for a variety of products. You have probably been pulled into what they call online funnels that turn an ad into a long-form sales page that leads you to a webinar or free report to download. From there they invite you to buy a product, register for an event or schedule a call.

They have refined the art and science of this to such a degree that many of them apply their same system to selling just about anything, from consulting to supplements. It works at a scale that you can barely imagine. The masters in this craft - and it is a craft - earn hundreds of millions of dollars of profit from following a reliable process over and over.

They first start by understanding the customer they're selling to. They research their pain points, their demographics, and they build a detailed avatar. They craft plain language messaging (super important point here, as we are all making our messaging to our markets far too complicated). They figure out where they can connect with the eyeballs of their clearly identified target market, and they put a compelling message in front of those eyes.

Once they connect, they create an offer for the customer to buy. Or they get on the phone so specific needs can be understood so they can craft a proposal and close the sale.

They refine this system so that they know for every dollar they spend how much they will get back in sales and profit. Once they know that, they just slowly increase the spend and know exactly how much will come out the other side. Essentially, they build a 24/7 sales force that delivers a predictable number of ideal prospects to their door.

Do you wish your sales and marketing processes could run with this amount of reliability?

How would having this type of system in place change how you feel about your future prospects? How much less would you have to worry about if this was how the attract-and-sign side of your business functioned?

I am not suggesting that you replicate an online sales funnel for your business (though that might work extraordinarily well for some readers). What I want you to understand is that there is a science to be learned that, when applied to your business, can give you a steady stream of new prospects. Prospects that sales quotas, PR firms and "spray and pray" marketing efforts simply cannot provide. If you are serious about feeling in control of your business, then I suggest you start to learn about growth hacking and online funnels so you can apply the scientific approach to client acquisition in your business.

This is the modern way people are selling in a world where your clients are staring at screens and have minutes (if not seconds) to glance at what you are offering. This is the modern way for them to develop a system - a repeatable and reliable system - that allows a business to grow and scale profitably, with far less worry and doubt.

Another side benefit of a steady stream of new business is weeding out the problem clients and acquiring more of the ones you really want. So many businesses wrestle with clients that don't pay enough or that they aren't making enough profit from. Business owners wish they could be working only with their ideal customers. Sure you could just fire all of your bad customers, but we all know that those customers, at least in our minds, pay the bills.

One of the ways to fix this and build the confidence to only have clients you love is to know that you have enough new business coming in. The right profitable business with the right kind of customers who are paying you the right fees. Then you won't feel bad about saying goodbye to the customers that are hurting your business. This also gives you the confidence to have the hard conversations with marginal clients and tell them what needs to change to make the relationship work for you.

Understanding growth hacking is worth at least as much time as you have worked to understand the old way of selling and marketing. You know all those sales books you read about trial closes, countering objectives and asking for the business? Did they ever really work when focused on you? If they did, did you ever hear from the salesperson much after the one-time sale?

Getting a "black belt" in growth hacking would serve your business well. It is an expertise that will show up in your cash account.

The High Value of Faster Answers

In the movie *Molly's Game,* the principal character, Molly (played by Jessica Chastain) was a hopeful Olympic mogul skier before she tripped on a stick during trials. Her life evolves (or devolves, depending on your point of view) into becoming the creator of a high stakes poker game for the rich and famous. While running her game in New York, the now "it" poker game attracts some unsavory characters. Law enforcement jumps in and pressures Molly to give up secrets on her players or face a long jail sentence.

Molly's estranged father shows up right before her trial and proceeds to have a short, direct and life-altering conversation with her.

Her well-respected psychiatrist father tells her that he is going to do what therapy patients have wished their therapists would do for decades: just give her the answers. In fact, he promises three years of therapy in three minutes. (It is, after all, a movie.)

Armed with all he knows about her past, he proceeds to explain what compelled her to run card games, why she incorrectly thinks her father liked her the least, and why her failure at skiing was not the failure she made it be (it was simply a fluke and meant nothing else).

His direct statements create a breakthrough. Molly's father closes the scene by saying, "See how much you can accomplish when you do not charge by the hour?"

What does this have to do with your business?

In short, people want answers.

Think about your sales process and how you deliver your service. If the length of time you are taking to deliver your value is slowed because you will make more money by having a drawn-out process, then you are cheating your client and yourself. There are many industries that follow a model that creates more revenue by going slower. But there are not many clients that want you to go slower and charge them more. Fewer speed bumps, better business.

When I start working with a client, I have to do some digging before I can provide them the answers they want. There is a certain amount I need to learn about a business, the owner, their competitors and their industry before I can give them a practical strategy to fix whatever is holding them back. However long that takes it how long it should take. Dragging it out for any longer or waiting for my client to figure it out on their own diminishes the experience for everyone. (Like a therapist asking, "What do you think the reason you are like this might be?" when they know the answer.)

While getting to the answers matters, how quickly you can get there is just as important.

You know the famous quote by Henry Ford: "If I had asked people what they wanted, they would have said faster horses." The quote is used to show how customers have no idea what they want. But that misses the bigger point. Customers DID know what they wanted! They wanted to get where they wanted to go faster. Henry Ford's solution was an automobile. People want answers, as quickly as possible.

What if you could create more value in getting people answers and/or results faster than everyone else?

This is your opportunity to stop presenting your version of the same process your competitors offer.

- What if you could do the discovery, strategy, design and launch of a website in four to six weeks instead of four to six months?

- What if you were the lawyer that had a way to conclude a divorce in six weeks instead of the usual one to two years?

- What if you designed a process that allowed a business deal to close in weeks instead of months?

- What if your business coaching process took three months instead of years?

- What if you were a therapist who, after learning enough information, just gave your patients the answers to their problems?

You might charge less (although I would argue you could charge more). But you will create the capacity to handle many more clients, projects and transactions with the same number of people. You would also attract clients who are sick and tired of endless projects and engagements that cost them too much. Word-of-mouth would be off the charts.

If you have high expertise in what you do and are always looking to increase the mastery of your craft, you know most of the answers or how to get to them quickly. You know the information you need to deliver great work for your clients. I am willing to bet that with some effort, you could figure out ways to get the results much faster than you do today.

Nobody wants to spend years in therapy. They just think that is the only way it works.

Until someone decides to change their expectations. So, for the people you sell to, what are the expectations (in time and money) for getting the results they want?

How could you give them the answers in half of the time and turn that into your competitive advantage? What could you do if you stopped connecting your value to time?

Speed to the right answer is a seldom used but winning strategy.

The Secret to Great Marketing

> *"Ambition is the path to success.*
> *Persistence is the vehicle you arrive in."*
>
> - BILL BRADLEY

Persistence.

There. I just saved you months of marketing book reading and countless dollars as you burn through another group of marketing agencies that claim to have the next secret sauce.

Sure, you need to have a message that is rooted in a core purpose that means as much to the people inside your organization as it does to those you hope will become customers. But, other than that, the one thing you must have is persistence. And it is much harder than finding a new tagline or building a new website.

It's not sexy and it is not the latest fad. What works for the long haul rarely is.

As they say, overnight successes take a long time. And that is true for the success of your marketing messages. So why are we so consumed with changing them every year like a fresh coat of paint? It's obvious (and a worn cliche) that everyone is looking for the quick fix that will create a flood of new business and profits. ***But the secret is that there is no secret.***

So we let our impatience cause our company to change our approach and message so often that we soon have none at all. At least not one anyone remembers.

So find that pure and simple message that fits your business and then simply prove it again and again. Not for the next few months or quarters. For years. The ways you prove it can change and evolve over time. You should never stop finding every possible way to make your message real to your customers. That is where marketing momentum and results will come from. Not from the message itself.

Stand for something great. Figure out the best way to say it. Keep saying it and proving it. For years. And years.

Persistence.

Look Better Naked

"Look better naked" was the tagline for David Barton Gym when it opened in New York City over 20 years ago. It remains one of the best taglines I have ever come across. It's not the shock value that is so great, per se. It is great because every other gym sells and markets with their lowest price, or membership specials, or having the most classes or best equipment.

"Look better naked" focuses FIRST on a very specific result/benefit that many of the people really want. What's more, it hits the marketing daily-double as it speaks to the benefit of the benefit. You'll be healthy and you'll look better naked in front of someone you want to impress. (Except, of course, the vain demographic that is merely interested in how they look at themselves in the mirror.)

David Barton built one of the most beautiful gyms in the city. It had the very latest equipment and elite personal trainers. But they did not market that up front because none of it mattered if they could not first make a connection with their ideal clientele. Then, and only then, could they show them what they had built to make their promise real.

Every ad they ran, every mailer they sent out and even their memberships stuck to this core idea. It was on the front of their t-shirts. Their trainers trained using a super slow motion approach that put a premium on aesthetic results. They baked their tagline into everything so that every interaction provided proof.

Now (no really, now) go read through the first page of your website (or even just the top section), your brochure and/your marketing material. Go read over your latest sales proposal or bid. Extra credit: Go read through the top section of several competitors' websites.

(I'll wait here. Cue the Jeopardy theme song...)

I am willing to wager that the language you are using across every sales touchpoint refers to what *you* do and how great you are at doing it. Maybe you even have clients saying nice things about you. You, you and you.

Like the person at the party talking your ear off about themselves who stops and says, "Enough about me, what do YOU think about me?" This is how 90% of businesses market and sell.

I have been guilty of it myself. Parts of my website still have some of me, me and me. It is not easy. We are proud of our businesses. We want people to be attracted to all that we do, our expertise and how much better we think we are than our competitors.

I hate to break it to you, but **our vanity, disguised as a persuasion technique, is slowing us down.**

Not only does it weaken our sales efforts, but it also makes us sound like everyone else. If you look at your competitors' core messages you will see how similar they all are.

Here in this giant sea of same lies the opportunity for us to completely transform our sales approach and our results. We must intrigue people by immediately letting them know what we will do for THEM.

Them, them and them.

Do you know the results your clients are craving? (Not just what they would like but what they crave?) If not, task number one is to start asking enough of them until it becomes crystal clear.

If you know what your clients crave, then it should be the only thing they see first on your website, your marketing material and 90% of your proposals or bids.

The ideal is for you to figure out how you will make them money, save them money, or both. For a business, both of those can be measured. They are not "soft" promises. As long as you are able to prove it, you should be able to show a prospect a solid estimate of how much money it will mean to them.

Want to make them a pretty website? Welcome to selling a commodity in 2018. Build them a website that will grow sales by 10, 15 or 25% next year and watch your sales take off.

Helping HR leaders communicate and improve internal communications is a soft benefit. The result of better internal communications and employee engagement is lower turnover (big savings in hiring/firing costs) and increased productivity (revenue and profit). The same service was just presented as a measurable result.

There is a tangible benefit to the buyer of every product or service. Find yours.

Be the company that is relentlessly focused on that benefit. Design everything around it and focus your innovation towards perfecting it.

Nobody will come and see the beautiful gym you built if they first do not understand why they should take a look.

Nothing makes business more fun to run than winning a lot of the right new clients. If you have the awareness to stop talking about yourself (a twist on fuck your pride) and the courage to change the conversation, you can improve the impact you make for your ideal clients.

How do you help your clients look better naked?

Hit the Blue Up!

> *"Simplicity is the most difficult thing to secure in this world; it is the last limit of experience and the last effort of genius."*
>
> - GEORGE SAND

UPS has over 108,000 delivery vehicles, 650 aircraft (owned or leased) and over 430,000 employees across the globe. Over the years they have developed one of the most sophisticated handheld devices ever made. They call it the Delivery Information Acquisition Device, DIAD for short. It is the instant entry point for a tracking system that averages over 101 million tracking requests every day.

So how do you put such a complicated device in the hands of so many people without bringing the company to a crawl, or opening a small university to train everyone? Answer: Make the interface dead simple.

Every time I see those DIAD devices in the hands of my UPS delivery person it reminds me of an experience I had with a UPS driver over 15 years ago. As I watched him click away with extraordinary speed and precision at the array of buttons on this intimidating device, I had to ask him, "How hard is that thing to use?" What he showed me has stuck with me ever since. On the small monochromatic screen, just above a set of big blue up/down arrows were the words **"Hit the blue up,"** telling him exactly what to do next. "It's great," he said, "totally dumbed down."

He did not say "dumbed down" in a negative way. He was clearly proud about his proficiency on this complex piece of electronics that anyone would be overwhelmed by at first (or tenth) glance. The story has stuck in my mind because that phrase, "dumbed down," continues to come up so often over the years.

When I tell this story to clients, audiences or prospects the response I often hear is: "No, I don't want to dumb it down. Our customers are smarter, more savvy, more…"

When we work on marketing, new products, business ideas, websites, presentations, etc., we spend a lot of time making sure that everything sounds as complicated as it can be. Complicated has come to equal uniqueness. Why? The more complex we can make our offerings (or make them sound that way) the more differentiated we will be. I believe the opposite to be true. Now more than ever.

When we get worried about dumbing something down, it is OUR intelligence that we are looking to protect. It is our ego, disguised as pride, wanting to prove our smarts. (You already know <u>what I think you should do</u> with your pride.)

Do you think the UPS driver thinks the IT group has dumbed things down for him? Or does extreme simplification make the cumbersome more manageable? When someone visits your website and there is language that makes each move incredibly clear, do you think the visitor feels insulted? Fewer hurdles to understanding, better speed of sales and services.

When someone can understand what you are offering and why they should care instantly, they will be more inclined to move forward with you.

The challenge we all face is to make something so incredibly powerful, VALUABLE and complex - like the UPS DIAD - yet make it so extraordinarily accessible that it takes seconds for the user to put that power to use.

Whether it is a multibillion dollar global communication system or making the value you provide to the market extraordinarily clear, you are not insulting anyone's intelligence by making it simple. You simply removed a giant obstacle to creating an action or making a sale.

Whatever it is you are offering, selling or trying to convey, no matter how complex it may be, how do you explain it as easily as: **"Hit the blue up"?**

Your employees, customers and prospects are busy. They no longer like to do a lot of reading (if they ever did) and they want to understand what is in it for them in as short a time as possible.

Do yourself a favor and **dumb it down for them.**

HOW COULD
YOU DO LESS TO
CHANGE YOUR
FORTUNES?

Burger, Fries and Shakes

The diner in a sleepy town outside of New York City is painfully empty, like too many other stores or restaurants you walk by these days. No doubt this struggle causes incredible stress to the owner of each business, leaving them way too much time to consider all the extra things they could try to change their fortunes.

But let's turn those thoughts around. How could you do LESS to change your fortunes (i.e. *Fewer Better*)? Consider that people actually do NOT want more from you and would welcome you giving them an amazingly great and simple moment. If there ever was a time that the saying, "longing for simpler times" rings true, it is our current moment.

So why can't that diner end the stress that comes from maintaining the enormous menu that tries to please everyone? What if they just focused on making PERFECT burgers, fries and shakes? Every ounce of energy focused into a finite offering that will be extraordinary.

No more. No less.

In the process, they will have reinvented their business. They will have found a way to be different from their competitors.

They will have found a way to have people start talking about them again and spreading the word. Not from that extra mailer or ugly banner with a "buy one get one free" offer. Just connect to what people went to diners for in simpler times - and deliver it with perfection.

The Shake Shack does just that, and the lines run around the block...and back. They are now a global public company that is, primarily, famous for a great burger, tasty fries and an amazing milkshake.

And it is true for every business.

What did "simpler times" in your industry look like?
What is the Burger, Fries and Shake of your industry?
Of your specific business?
Are they the absolute best anyone could ever find?

Reaching the Top 3% of Your Industry

Now that we have talked about a lot of sales and marketing strategies, I want to give you the simplest one of all. A game plan that will do more for the longevity of your business than all of the marketing, sales and strategy books (including this one) combined.

After many years of listening to businesses, experiencing the service they provide, and working with them to get things done, I have come up with the one thing that will put your business in the top 3% of whatever industry you are in. Here it is ....(drumroll) ...

Do what you said you would do. Do it when you said you would do it.

There it is. Seems so simple. And yet how many interactions and experiences have you had where you can count on it? How many follow-ups do you send to people? How many are you responding to? How many letters, emails and calls are you making and receiving with apologies for deadlines and promises missed?

When I stick to this rule, clients come to me. You may want more magic, but there it is.

Businesses, lost in a fog of promises not kept, long to find a company to work with that makes this simple rule real. When I forget it, I lose credibility, create stress for myself and my clients, and fall back into the blur of the crowd.

Do what you said you would do. Do it when you said you would do it. Your competition is not talking about it. Your clients and prospects cannot wait to hear it. What are the steps you need to put in place so it becomes the rule your business NEVER breaks? When?

Put it on your business cards, on the first slide of your presentation, and at the top of every mission statement.

Welcome to the top 3% of your industry.

**Extra credit:

Do more than what you said you would do. Still do it when you said you would.

Welcome to the top **1%** of your industry.

DO MORE
THAN WHAT
YOU SAID YOU
WOULD DO.

RISK & RESILIENCE

> "
>
> FAMILIAR
> PAIN IS THE
> DEVIL. JUMP
> OUT OF IT!

Don't Boil Like a Frog

You probably know the fable of the boiling frog. A frog dropped in boiling water will immediately leap out. But if you put that same frog in cool water and slowly bring it to a boil it will stay in the water until it dies.

I'm thinking about two initial conversations with two established business owners. These are business owners who have built meaningful businesses over several years. After they each told me the standard intro about their companies, I asked a question that does not usually get asked in a business context: "You have been running this business now for many years. How do you feel?" After some surprise and then a long pause, I heard about how the early years were filled with growth and the past three to five years have been, for lack of a better word, flat. Revenue has stayed the same or dropped a bit. Profit was not moving. It had been this way for enough years that the owners' view of the future was now only some variant of this known past. They did not feel good about it, but both chalked it up to being just the way it is.

Business should be a struggle, right?

I have had this conversation, in different ways, with dozens of business owners. Some businesses are doing marginally well but not at the level that is close to their potential. The business owners are not happy but have become used to this level of frustration.

They are all slowly being brought to a boil and do not see it. Yet.

You see, frogs do not have the market cornered on staying put despite growing discomfort. We humans, despite (or maybe because of) our bigger brains, habitually **choose known pain over unknown change.**

I have endured years of known pain at different times in my life and career. In retrospect, you can barely perceive the protracted and subtle descent. After years of slogging through the recession of the 90's, I needed someone else to tell me that I had lost my smile to even recognize how resigned I had become to the struggle. It had simply become my normal. It never should have been.

There is a well-studied phenomenon that when pain becomes familiar, letting go of that pain can actually cause more of it. After all, we have grown accustomed to what we know. Leaving it behind for something new can feel like leaping off a bridge, even if we realize that the leap will likely take us to a better place. American scientist Jared Diamond calls it "creeping normality." It is how major change can be accepted as normal if it happens slowly enough. Making small steps towards positive change is the constructive version of this phenomenon. But sadly, many of us also accept creeping normality when it moves us to stasis or slow decline.

I have been thinking about this dilemma because I am in the

business of igniting massive change for business owners and their businesses. Why is the promise of a better future not a big enough catalyst, especially when compared to a stagnant business? It reminded me of *Willy Wonka and the Chocolate Factory*. You know the scene where Charlie Bucket is flying over the village and Mr. Wonka turns to him and says, "Don't forget what happened to the man who suddenly got everything he always wanted. He lived happily ever after."

Sometimes we fear getting everything we ever hoped for. Do I really want to have it all? Wouldn't the pain of losing it all be horrific? Why in the world would I want to ride that roller coaster? Why can't we leap for everything that we always wanted? **Why not you?**

So we sit in the pots of our own making and simmer. In many cases, things will get to a point where the pain is so great that the risks seem so bad and we make a move. But it's way too late. More often, the pain never gets too great and we waste a decade... or five.

Given this, how can we change our thinking about where we are and where we truly want to be? How do we propel ourselves into making the leap to the business that fuels the life we want?

If you want a different outcome, try a different approach:

1 **"How do you feel?"** That question demands an answer, even if you are asking it of yourself. Is your business what you wanted it to be? **How long have you been accepting the status quo? How long will you give the status quo such exclusive status?**

Bring these thoughts out from the back of your mind and into a place that forces you to deal with them. Write about your particular case of status quo and how long you have been locked in it.

2 **Think bigger!** What would it take to double your business in the next three years? Double the profit and, with it, your income? What would your life be like when that became real? What could you do that you cannot do today?

Write it in vivid and measurable detail. The specific profit number, the number of new clients you will have and the average fee/annual revenue you will earn from each. When every year is just a little bit better than the year before, we lose sight of any outcome that can be more audacious.

Now reverse engineer that result into the smallest possible steps you can take in the next month. Big goals are great to talk about but they can become overwhelming. Too many things to do and too much to juggle in our minds. Set that big goal and then take 1,000 small steps. With determination.

3 **What are the risks?** Make a list of everything that scares you about this larger future. What could go wrong? What could you lose? Now, next to each risk, write one or two strategies that could mitigate it.

Tony Robbins points out that most suffering is due to a fear of loss, fear of less, or fear of never. If you think about the downsides that we most worry about, you will see they are often connected to *losing something/everything,* having *less than before,* or the fear of trying and *never getting what we want.*

Get clear on what risks are holding you back, then take away their power by thinking through solutions for each.

4 **Do it anyway.** When you are afraid, your subconscious is alerting you to the risks involved in leaving your comfortable pain behind. It does not need any more help from you. What is needed is the space and time to let your cognitive brain think rationally so your fears and worries don't stop your progress.

It is possible you will endure some more pain in the process of getting what you really want. Do it anyway. You may lose some revenue as you ditch lousy clients so you have time to work with ideal clients. Do it anyway.

The reasons you will come up with to not get out of your known pain will be limitless. Do it anyway.

5 **Fuck your pride and ask for help.** In order to get out of a rut, you need clarity about what is keeping you in it. As I like to say, it is hard to read the label when you are stuck inside the bottle. Find someone who can see more clearly than you, then actively listen to what they say. If you could have done it all alone you would have done it by now. Remember the person who told me that I had lost my smile? That nudge (more like a slap) flipped my normal to unacceptable. Everything changed for me and the business after that.

We all need a leg up if we want to do something truly great. But you have to be willing to ask for, and be receptive to, help.

You know the phrase, "Better the devil you know than the one you don't?" It assumes that the unknown is evil. Consider that you get to decide what the unknown means to you. So what will you choose?

Familiar pain is the devil. It is painful but tolerable hot water. Jump out of it!

The Man in the Arena

"It is not the critic who counts: not the man who points out how the strong man stumbles or where the doer of deeds could have done better. The credit belongs to the man who is actually in the arena, whose face is marred by dust and sweat and blood, who strives valiantly, who errs and comes up short again and again, because there is no effort without error or shortcoming, but who knows the great enthusiasms, the great devotions, who spends himself for a worthy cause; who, at the best, knows, in the end, the triumph of high achievement, and who, at the worst, if he fails, at least he fails while daring greatly, so that his place shall never be with those cold and timid souls who knew neither victory nor defeat."

- Theodore Roosevelt

"

THE FEAR
IS IN THE
WAITING.

Doing Harm to Your Business On Purpose

> "Decisions. We can think about things, turn them over in our minds a million times, play out possible scenarios. But really when it comes down to it, you have to go with your heart and move forward. Maybe things will go well. Maybe they'll turn out poorly. Every decision brings with it some good, some bad, some lessons, and some luck. The only thing that's for sure is that indecision steals many years from many people who wind up wishing they'd just had the courage to leap."
>
> – DOE ZANTAMATA

The certainty of the negative without equal certainty of the positive keeps businesses frozen in time.

The one question that comes up the most when I am speaking with entrepreneurs who have been in business for a while is: How do I fire bad clients without killing my business?

It is easy to say to just get rid of them. But we all know that means a drop in revenue, profit and often a reduction in expenses (and staff as part of that) as an offset. I have given a variety of answers and strategies, but none are truly satisfying because the implications to the business are often severe and point to a much larger issue.

How do you make a decision that will hurt your business in the short term without 100% (or even 80%) certainty that it will help in the long term?

How do you make the leap of faith to damage your business in order to make it better?

Maybe you have clients that cost you more than you earn from them. Maybe the market is shifting under your feet and you need to make a big investment to change how you do business. Maybe you need to make some key new hires to allow you to handle larger clients long before the revenue from those larger clients comes in.

How many of these decisions are you putting off? How long have you been struggling with the status quo? How bad does the pain have to be in your business before you make these hard decisions?

Here are a few better questions to consider:

How can I do everything I can to ensure the successful outcome after I make these hard decisions? (Execute, execute and... execute.)

How can I get more comfortable with the short term pain these moves will create so I can get through them with more ease?

The reason there is no perfect answer to the question, "What do I do with my bad clients?" is that the answer will involve some level of discomfort that you may or may not be ready for. The fear of self-inflicted damage to our business, despite it being the right thing to do, stops the decision. Cold.

With this in mind, I want you to think deeply about the downside you are worried about. How real is it? How long have you been putting it off and at what cost to you and your business? At what cost to your staff that has to deal with the bad clients? At what cost to morale? At what cost to the clients that you love?

Can you think through all the steps that will take you from the hard decision to the lasting change you want to make? How can you create a plan that minimizes the pain and gets as close as possible to guaranteed success? **And, when will you do it?**

If you take the time and space to meticulously think through the path to a much larger future for your business, but still will not take action to create it, then the only thing stopping you is fear.

If you will indulge me here a bit further, I want to share a helpful mantra: "Fear is in the waiting."

You may be familiar with ex-Navy Seal and author Jocko Willink and his book, *Extreme Ownership*. You may be less aware of his terrific children's book, *Way of the Warrior Kid*.

In *Way of the Warrior Kid,* a young boy is grappling with being bullied. He lacks confidence after a tough year of school. His Navy Seal Uncle comes to spend the summer and teaches the boy to swim. The culmination of this swimming instruction is a leap off of a bridge into a river. The young boy is frozen with fear, despite knowing that he is now a very strong swimmer. He has watched his uncle jump off the bridge many times so he knows it is safe and doable. His uncle explains to him that the fear he is feeling only exists in the waiting. The fear is from all the bad possible outcomes that are filling his mind, despite having done everything necessary to be ready for the jump.

The fear is in the waiting.

You may never be 100% sure about the outcome of the tough decisions you need to make to dramatically improve the future of your business. However, if you have done everything possible to prepare for the leap you know you must take, then the only thing stopping you is fear.

Put in the planning. Get comfortable with things being worse before they get better. Be confident in your plan.

Leap!

Growth and Comfort Cannot Coexist

> *"Feeling scared just means you're moving closer to growth."*
>
> - ROBIN SHARMA

In a recent interview, IBM CEO Ginni Rometty, told a story about being offered a promotion in her early days at IBM. While she felt she was not ready for the promotion, she was persuaded to take it. Her lesson from that experience hit a nerve:

"Growth and comfort cannot exist together."

And yet we yearn for comfort. In our lives and in how we want to run our businesses. We strive to reach the point where we feel that our business can run without us.

That is a trap!

I remember spending 15 months on a business turnaround. When the CFO informed us that the business was profitable again, it was a true and well deserved moment of celebration. But when the owners decided to then relax and just keep doing what was working... TRAP! When things get comfortable, it is a signal to stretch your thinking.

Ask yourself:

- What would you have to deliver to customers to charge twice what you charge today?

- If you would rate your current level of service at a 4, what would you need to do to deliver a service level of 10?

- Maybe you want to start to grow through acquisition. So start talking to capital advisors and thinking about team members that could work with you on that task.

Understand your comfort zone and push against it. You should not stay away from a new piece of business because you do not think you are ready for it. You should not just keep doing what you have been doing because it is working and it is comfortable.

Instead, get comfortable being uncomfortable.

Leave autopilot to pilots and their airplanes.

Someone is out there trying to steal your business. They are waiting for you to get comfortable and to stop growing. Nobody is immune to it.

Do you think locksmiths thought that someone was building a startup to disrupt their little niche copying keys? Then along comes KeyMe with 150 kiosks across New York City that will copy your key in 30 seconds. You can scan your key via their app and have it delivered. Locksmiths, disrupted. LOCKSMITHS!

Let's be clear, this is not about living a life of paranoia. This is not about worry. It is all about GROWTH! Professionally and personally.

It's about getting joy from the fact that you have a business that is never finished. One that pushes you to evolve, learn and expand. To keep improving skills and stay uncomfortable. To run a business that is constantly evolving. To lead your team to challenge themselves and evolve along with the business.

You get to live a life of continual growth and have a business that does the same. And that totally rocks!

Growth and comfort cannot exist together.

Pick one.

KEEP CALM.
TAKE ACTION.

Business Survival and Revival

> *"Choices are the hinges of destiny."*
>
> – EDWIN MARKHAM

The coronavirus pandemic has been the fourth such recession/shock/crash I have been through in my career. (Makes me feel a bit old writing that.) Many people are correctly saying that we will get through this together, and that everything will return to normal (I'm less sure about that). Given my background and the focus of my work, I want to share some important lessons I have learned, often the hard way, about managing businesses through crises both large and small.

My hope is to shake you by the shoulders so you will take decisive action today and not wait to see what happens. I also want to snap you out of feeling stuck or trapped by the uncertainty that surrounds the pandemic. While it may be right to, as the famous saying goes, "Keep calm and carry on," I would implore you to keep calm and *take action*. Without panic. Now.

There are two phases here. The first one is survival. IF you get the survival part right, you will be able to move on to revival.

Business Survival

In nearly every past crisis, the business I was running was not immediately impacted. So I felt relieved and I waited. Big mistake. When a good portion of any economy takes a shock it will eventually trickle down to you. Unless you are in the Purell, toilet paper or hospital masks/supplies business, fallout from the pandemic is going to hit you at some point. Harder than you think.

In the late '90s, corporate America was laying off employees in extraordinary numbers. My business just charged a small fee so I thought we would fall under the radar. I kept moving forward with business as usual. At some point, the CFOs of our clients could not cut any more staff and turned their attention to every other expense. Eventually they got to us. Competitors of all sizes were not waiting around like I was and had started offering fees 50-75% lower than what we were charging our clients. One by one our best clients came to show me these proposals and asked me to match it, or else. I complied, cursed my competitors. I made less revenue while my costs and work-load were the same. Crushing.

My competitors were right. They were reacting to what is and not what was. They went on the attack while I was hunkering down and hoping this would all pass. News alert: Hope is not a strategy.

My pride in my fees and clinging to a business structure that was no longer relevant were my weaknesses.

How much your market is changing right now is equal to how much opportunity exists right in front of you. Will you lament what was, or leap into what is? How you answer this question will tell me a lot about the fate of your business.

Let's get even more specific:

Know your numbers. You need a financial roadmap first so you know what must be done. Grab your CFO, bookkeeper or Quickbooks reports and model out what the rest of the year will look like for you. The worst-case scenario is a better place to start than wishful thinking. If you have not been totally shut down, there are moves you can make - even though they will require many hard choices - that will reduce your losses.

Over and over I have learned that waiting for a few months will generate losses that you cannot come back from. If there is something you think you can wait for a few months to do, please learn from my past pain and do it right away.

"How can I help?" This is the time to get on a video call with every one of your clients, prospects and vendors and ask two very simple questions: "How can I help?" and "What do you need?" Do not wait for them to call you to deliver bad news or question your fees. Be their partner in every possible way, even if they never thought of you that way.

You may need to help them for free for a while. You may need to slash your fees and costs or defer them. Do it. If you are proactive, you will have the chance to negotiate creative ways to make those fees back when things get better.

From this process, you will learn the economics and state of your market that is now your reality. You must use that reality to rapidly transform your business to take advantage of the new playing field.

Will you need to offer more service for the same price? Or the same service for half of the price? If your products or services have become obsolete, what else do customers need that you could deliver? If you can get clarity about what you are facing, then you can find creative solutions and attack the market based on what it needs.

$1.00 less. *Fewer Better expenses*. Fewer better expenses. Now combine your clear-eyed projections for your rest of the year revenues plus what your customers/clients are telling you. Your next move is to figure out how to make your expenses at least $1.00 less than that projected revenue number. How? Imagine every current employee and expense are pieces on a chess-board. Take them all off and put them to the side. Next, design a business that can operate for $1.00 less than your revenue. What positions do you need and what expenses are required? Now put only those chess pieces back on the board. The raw reality is that some pieces will not make it back to the board and that means letting people go. Years ago, with 150 in staff, I did this exercise with my CFO. We sat in the conference room late into the night until we eventually got there. If you have enough revenue, there is a version of your business that can spend at least $1.00 less than you take in. Find it and then make it real.

Your job right now is to save the company and as many jobs as you can. I know how hard laying people off is. I have had clients who felt there is more honor in everyone going down with the ship together. There isn't.

By resetting the business for the worst-case scenario means you only have to do this once. Slowly cutting staff a little at a time destroys morale. Get it all over with and then you can explain to your team why you had to make these changes and how you will all work together to get things moving in a better direction.

Constraints force innovation. My old business charged an average of $120 per transaction. When a crisis hit, it was clear to me that our fees were going to drop to $60 per transaction for the exact same work. I could yell about how that was not valuing our work. Or I could figure out how to have a business that could deliver superior service at $60, with profit. When I finally *got over my pride* and answered that question, it generated a novel approach to using the internet that increased our productivity by a factor of 10.

When nobody is questioning your fees or asking you to increase efficiency, you keep rolling along with the status quo. If you rethink your business as if you were starting it today, you will be amazed at how many savings and inefficiencies you have been ignoring. I did this with a client last year and saved over $3 million dollars in expenses by focusing the business's strengths. AND we increased the level of service to customers.

Business Revival

Attack. Now that you know you are going to survive, it is time to make noise about your faster, more innovative business. In the same way that the world's best investors will tell you this is the time to buy stocks, now is also the time to invest in your business. How can you position your business to go on offense? That new service you have been wanting to offer? Launch it. All the content you know you should be putting out so more potential clients know about you? Write it, record it and spread it across social media. You will likely have 3 or 4 months of a real lull to do it. Now is the time.

If you aggressively increased efficiency and lowered your costs, you may be able to go after new business with a lower fee. Better yet, use the constraints of this moment to innovate a whole different pricing model that your potential clients desperately need right now.

Disrupt your own business. As if you were the rebel outsider aiming to topple every company that is not taking action to change at this moment.

Let me say it again: the survival and revival of your business will depend on whether you aggressively reshape your business to the world *as it will be,* not try to operate some smaller version of your old business through these times.

Some say everything will come roaring back as soon as we hear this pandemic is under control. But we have never experienced this type of crisis before, and I am certain that nothing will be the same.

This shock will leave a long echo. Long after this is over, businesses will have realized they can operate with a lot less staff and with lower expenses. They will not be so quick to just add them all back on.

Once clients taste a lower fee they will be less open to raising it later. They will have learned the power of putting pressure on expenses and will continue to do so for some time to come. While over the long haul it may change back as they get fat again, it is many years away, so do not bet your business on a speedy recovery.

I know reading all of this is not reassuring, but I am not a rainbows and unicorns kind of guy when it comes to business. I desperately want every business to survive this and I have 20+ years of experience that tells me what actually works.

1. Know your real numbers.

2. $1.00 less.

3. Get connected to your customers.

4. Wipe the chessboard clean.

5. Reshape your business based on what will be. (Constraints create innovation!)

6. Attack!

I am certain you can do all of the steps I outlined above. Will you do it today and get it done this week? It all comes down to speed and determination to do what must be done.

Keep calm. Take action.

> "
>
> WE'VE ALL GOT
> A BLACK BOOK
> OF MISSED
> OPPORTUNITIES.

Keep Pulling the String

> *"All the roads you regret for not going to
> the end represent the alternative lives
> you have missed!"*
>
> - MEHMET MURAT ILDAN

The perfectly bound book slid out of the FedEx envelope. Stamped
in silver foil on the cover was the name of the prestigious investment bank that had sent it to me. I remember thinking to myself,
"Wow. This is the real deal!" And, "What the hell am I doing?"

Just days earlier, the same investment bank had sent me a
cryptic letter explaining that they were representing a smaller
niche competitor of mine that was looking to be acquired. Based
on not much more information than that, they asked if I would be
interested in signing a confidentiality agreement so they could
send me the "book" they had prepared.

Curiosity fully piqued, I signed away.

Now it was here. A hundred plus pages all about a company
that would cost five or six million dollars to acquire. For some of
you, that may not seem like a large number, but at that moment

in time my business was losing money, surviving on a large bank credit line, and had exactly zero dollars to put towards an acquisition of any size.

As I flipped through the pages, a story unfolded of a company that was an incredible match for the short and long-term strategy of my business. Their offices all overlapped where I had offices and there were many other synergies.

But five or six million dollars??

Who was I kidding?

Whether it was youth, naivete, stupidity - or a healthy combination of all three - I decided to take the next step. There was a tiny thread there that intrigued me so I decided to keep pulling on it until the business gods (or my bank) forced me to stop.

I flew out to L.A. and met with the investment bankers and the owner. We hit it off. Check.

I had a great phone call with their main investor. Check.

I spent a week flying around the U.S. meeting one-on-one with all the key executives. Check.

We agreed on a price of just over five million dollars, two million of which had to be paid at closing.

Now, If you have been paying attention, I did not have $20,000 much less two million to pay to anyone.

But the string I was pulling was getting pretty long now. I could not stop myself from pulling.

So I created my own little book.

A concise narrative and a set of spreadsheets that showed what the combined companies would look like at closing and over the next five years after that.

I asked some friends in the investment banking space if they knew of someone to talk to who might lend or invest the money. I had no right to raise this much money but why not just see what happens if I tried?

The first banker I met with told me they only do deals of $10 million and over. She gave me two references that might be a better fit.

Then this next batch said it was too big for them, or too small… But gave me two more people to call.

Meeting after meeting, more than 40 Goldilocks "too hot or too cold" moments like this came and went. Each time, I refined my pitch and my numbers. I got better at learning how the entire system works.

Finally, one of those generous referrals paid off. I had found a small investment bank that had a fund that was looking for deals exactly like mine. Our poor balance sheet did not scare them away, and they loved (or at least were comfortable with) my short and long term plan.

VICTORY!

With the $2 million secured, we forged ahead to drafting documents and working on a transition plan. To my DAILY amazement, this looked like this deal was actually going to happen. A deal that would flip us into profitability and transform our position in the market.

Two weeks before closing, the owner of the company invited me to come to his vacation home for lunch. Off I went, excited to be able to discuss our future together, world domination, etc., etc.

It turns out, he actually asked me to come there to tell me he had developed cold feet and decided he did not want to sell the business to me - or to anyone.

Defeat. Total defeat.

Wait, what the fuck??

I hear you... "Howard, why did you just spend 741 words telling me about an epic business LOSS?" Great question!

I tell you this story because it is one of my most memorable business experiences and lessons. I see it as one of my biggest victories. (After the weeks of total heartbreak and sadness, of course.)

Though I did not make the acquisition, I gained something that turned out to be far more valuable. A real-life experience, knowledge, contacts and new skills that I could have not learned any other way.

But the biggest lesson of all has been this...

Keep pulling the string.

Time and again, my clients explain to me various opportunities they are presented with and, before taking ANY action, decide how each opportunity will end and why they have no business pursuing it.

Time and again, they can explain to me the future they wish they could have for their business and their life and, in the SAME breath, explain to me all of the reasons it will never happen for them.

Somehow, we magically know the outcome of our business even though we cannot possibly know anything more than the next quarter or year. (This pandemic should have proved this to you.)

Twenty-two years ago, I knew very little about acquisitions, raising capital or the legal aspects of these types of larger deals. Somehow, maybe from desperation, I decided to pull on the string that started as nothing more than a simple cryptic letter.

Every time I pulled that thread a little bit more, I got a crash course in raising money, acquiring businesses and dealing with the many, many bumps along the dealmaking road.

Investment bankers were generous in sharing feedback on my pitch and even more generous in sharing their contacts. I learned how to manage the many moments where deals look like they will fall apart and ways to get deals back on track. I built a network of bankers that I would work with and refer others to for YEARS. These bankers now knew I was looking to acquire businesses and started to send ME more deals.

I completed five other acquisitions after this one bombed and have helped countless clients acquire or sell their businesses using bits and pieces of what I learned from this one failed deal.

NONE of it would have happened if I did not push myself to pull that first small thread.

So now I ask you, where have there been threads that you have decided not to pull because you thought you knew where they would end? In the words of English actor Jim Broadbent, "We've all got a black book of missed opportunities."

Lots of people talk about missed opportunities. Looking back, we usually missed them because we decided up front where an opportunity would lead even though we had absolutely NO idea.

If I am honest with myself, I have missed opportunities because I was worried about trying and failing. Of having an outcome that would have hurt my pride. Of seeming foolish or convincing myself it would be a big waste of time.

Some of those reasons even make sense as I write them. But if they were true, why would missed opportunities be SO connected with regret?

Here is a challenge for you: Take out a piece of paper and write down past opportunities where you decided they would not work out before you even took a teeny, tiny step forward.

Is there a common theme to them? Is there a common fear?

How could you rewrite that theme (or counter that fear) so it would work better for you? Write it down.

What would have been the real harm if you had decided to pull the string a bit and see where it would have led you? Write that down too.

I pulled a string, was left at the business wedding altar, and, because I saw the opportunity all the way through to the end, I have no regrets.

The next time a seemingly out-of-reach opportunity appears, I hope you see it as a tiny thread that could lead to an incredible experience, and that you give that string a little pull.

WHEN YOUR
BUSINESS IS
HURTING, SO
ARE YOU.

Before We Say Goodbye

I have shared a lot of strategies and lessons in the preceding stories. Before I leave you I want to share two stories that are far more important than sales, marketing, profits and business. They are about how we view the bad things that happen to us, the importance of resilience, and the power of gratitude for what we have now vs. always wishing for a better future.

These are the stories I tell myself often. They are not dessert - they are the main meal reasons we attend to our businesses so passionately. I want to tell you why all the principles of *Fewer Better* that I've outlined in the book matter so much to me on a personal level.

If you own a business, there is no separation between business and your life. I know there is much written about work/life balance but it is akin to the mythical fountain of youth. It doesn't exist.

When your business is hurting, so are you. When you are hurting, your business will too.

So how we think about and manage the bad and appreciate the good things that are part of life AND business are directly connected to the type of business and life we allow ourselves to lead.

With that in mind, here are two final and important lessons that have helped me and my clients reframe those hard times.

The Broken Places

*"The world breaks everyone and afterward
many are stronger at the broken places."*

- ERNEST HEMINGWAY

I wish I could remember where I first heard the above Hemingway quote. I remind myself of it often and have shared with countless friends and clients over the years.

As I thought about the fallout from 2020, I was reminded of it again.

The quote resonates with me because, if you have lived a while (I am in my 54th year on this planet - yikes!), the world will kick you in the teeth, or much further south, and try to break you.

Over my 30+ year career, I have owned businesses that teetered on the brink of bankruptcy, had relationships fail, felt the stress of my child enduring pain, and felt the deep sorrow from the loss of loved ones.

Several years ago, my marriage ended, my income plummeted and I lost someone close to me after a long battle with cancer - all within the span of six months.

It broke me. In a lot of places.

By the end of it all, I had unintentionally lost over 30 pounds and vividly remember sitting on my couch, collapsed, and thoroughly defeated, just staring out of the window. Frozen in a fog of fear and sadness.

I have always considered myself to be a resilient person and had been knocked down before. But this was a lot all at once. How was I going to bounce back?

Then I remembered the Hemingway quote.

I found a way to turn those hard times into lessons learned. New wisdom, learned only by going through the toughest of times, would become part of my superpowers. These experiences would create guardrails so I could create a future that would be strengthened by my past, not burdened by it. (SO much easier to say now than it was to do.)

We can choose to feel broken or less-than because of what has happened to us, or we can see that we are stronger because we have been broken.

What a beautiful thing it is to be able to stand tall and say, "I fell apart, and I survived."

Five years later, I have completed the successful turnaround of an amazing boutique real estate development company, coaching a few business owners that are going through tough times, and have some exciting creative endeavors that satisfy the craftsperson in me. I am closer to friends that have always been there for me. And, most of all, my son is thriving.

The broken man (or Mann, in this case) on the couch was not actually broken. I was just looking at it all the wrong way.

How are you looking at the moments that break you?

Time and again, friends and clients explain to me the ways the world has broken them. How they would never trust again or could not believe their business could succeed. That the cracks or wounds life had dealt them would never heal. That these wounds would forever make them unable to love or be loved, or to succeed.

That they would be seen as a broken person or a bad business person.

Every new failed relationship would be used as further proof.

Every bad thing that happened in their business would be an example that they were cursed.

This is when I send them the quote.

Then we discuss it for as long and as often as it takes until they believe it.

Kintsugi Pottery - Broken is Beautiful

Kintsugi is a centuries-old Japanese art of fixing broken pottery with tree sap infused with gold, silver or platinum powder. The end result is a repaired piece that highlights the broken cracks and is even more beautiful and brilliant than the original.

Let me repeat that: What is broken and put back together is even more beautiful than the original.

2020 was a non-stop barrage of shattering events. Maybe your business has been crushed, your relationships tested by being stuck inside, maybe you have endured the fear that you, or those close to you, would catch COVID. Or maybe you lost someone to this horrible disease.

Where you go from here depends on how you decide to view the cracks this year has created - as well as the cracks you have been carrying from all the years before this one.

Will they define you? Or will you see them as your sources of strength and beauty?

Life is hard.

I remember an old holiday card my father got me as a teen-ager that read, "Life is tough, life is hard... Here's your fucking Christmas card." (My father has a warped sense of humor, and the apple fell right next to that tree.)

Life IS tough. Life IS hard. But you are stronger because of it.

I hope you will use this strength to rebuild, do more and make the coming years times of growth, renewal and happiness for you and your family.

"Every adversity, every failure, every heartache carries with it the seed of an equal or greater benefit."

– NAPOLEON HILL

> REGRET ONLY
> EXISTS IN THE
> REARVIEW
> MIRROR. DON'T
> LOOK BACK.

I Am the Luckiest Guy in the World

I have a son with a generous heart, a gentle soul and a wicked-smart sense of humor. He makes me smile with the type of smile that builds from deep inside like nothing else in my life.

I get to live in arguably one of the greatest cities in the world - New York City - and I feel fortunate to have grown up here. I have traveled the world and had experiences that very few have had.

My friends, family and clients come to me for help with their most difficult challenges and confide in me about their most guarded fears. I help them better enjoy their work and life. That people I care about and respect trust me to be in their corner is an honor.

I live in a time where the only limit to what I can achieve is how brave I can be at attempting things, even when they scare me to my core.

I often forget to think about how lucky that makes me. I always want more, or I obsess about what could/should have been. I am doing myself a disservice. Human nature is a tough opponent.

I can hear you... "Why is this the conclusion to a book about business strategy and marketing?"

Fair question. My answer? The conversations we are having about our businesses and our lives are coming from the wrong place. We yearn for more in our business because we are unhappy with where we are in the rest of our lives. We rarely stop to appreciate how far we have come, what it took to get here and what we have right now. We think that striving for more is a badge of honor. That we are being measured by others against how they perceive our hustle.

We look back with regret about what we could have done instead of what has been achieved, learned and experienced.

Regret is a choice. We choose it too often.

The final scene of the movie *Field of Dreams* chokes me up no matter how many times I see it. You know the scene. Ray Kinsella, played by Kevin Costner, realizes all of his work has brought him face to face with his father when he was a young man. (Brought back to life via the magic of the baseball field he built in the middle of his Iowa corn farm.) All of his regrets about his relationship with his dad culminate in him asking him to **have a catch.** A simple act he wishes he did more of when he was young.

For me, it brings back memories of playing catch with my father and all the dynamics of a father/son relationship. Now that I am a father, it makes me think about prioritizing my time with my son while he still likes hanging out with his dad.

But the bigger lesson is about holding on to so much regret. Regrets create sadness and frustration. Truth be told, everyone has them, myself included.

I sometimes spend time thinking about things I could have done differently 19 years ago when I owned my freight business. Friendships that slipped away. Decisions I made that did not go as planned. I can look at it all with regret, or I can look at it as an opportunity to learn and not repeat the same mistakes.

Our memories allow us to relive too many moments in our past and marry them with the knowledge we have in the now. That is a disjointed and unfair feedback loop. It's ammunition for your pride to kick you in the head.

"If only I knew then what I know now" is the chorus of the song of regret.

For those of us who cannot build a magical baseball field where we get to go back and fix our regrets, we need to find a way to change how we think about them.

Regrets simply do not serve us.

These stories of perceived failure, and the meaning we have given them, is a choice we make alone. Since it is a choice, then we can choose what those stories actually mean to us. We can also choose, just as easily, to look back and remember all the successes.

When I stop the regret stories in my mind, I make a choice to think of them as lessons. I then use my memory and current knowledge to craft rules and solutions that form guardrails for my life and my work.

No, I do not live in a magical world filled with only laughter and picnics. I doubt you do either. There is unimaginable tragedy in life. Moments of profound pain. Long periods of sustained stress and worry.

A last instruction from me: Grab a piece of paper and write down everything you have achieved so far. No setbacks or regrets. Just what you have achieved in your life and your career. Go as far back as you will let yourself. How lucky or fortunate do you feel when you read it? If not, why do you choose to see it that way? How could you see it differently?

Once you have your list, put it in your phone or on a piece of paper so you can read it each morning. Think about the lessons you learned from it all.

My path to feeling like the luckiest man in the world started when I began to reframe the question, "How did I let that happen?" as "What was the lesson of what happened?"

Those lessons have turned into a few books, keynotes and dozens of businesses that I helped to not make the same mistakes that I did. I have tried to share my lessons in ways that help others take actions so they will have fewer regrets.

As I write this, I am planning a vacation with my son. We will have some laughs. I hope to share some lessons with him. He will teach me a few things. We'll create new memories. **And very likely we'll even have a catch.**

I hope your business has taught you many valuable lessons. Lessons that, if you allow them, will create better relationships and a better future for you, those you care about and your business.

Your journey is unfolding in front of you and the possibilities are without limit. Regret only exists in the rearview mirror. Don't look back.

And when holidays, weekends, and time off come, do the things that bring you joy, with no regrets.

Fewer.
Better.